NATHAN FEILES, LCSW-R

GRASS IS

GREENER

SYNDROME

Relationships, Commitment, Perfectionism,
and the Life-Changing Fear of Missing Out

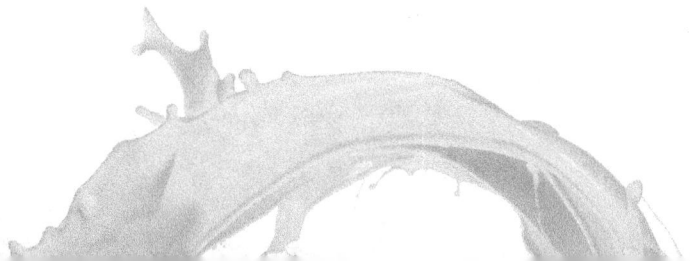

TABLE OF CONTENTS

INTRODUCTION

People often ask how I became interested in exploring and research-ing Grass Is Greener Syndrome. To answer this question, I should first explain a bit about who I am and my background as a therapist.

I completed my graduate studies with an MSW at New York University (NYU) and trained post-graduate for four years at the National Institute for the Psychotherapies in New York City, earn-ing a certificate in comprehensive psychotherapy and contemporary psychoanalysis (I'm a relational psychoanalyst and an integrative psychotherapist, as I have a background in working with various therapy modalities). Early on, I earned my field and licensing hours providing psychotherapy in community mental health, and also at the NYU counseling center for graduate and undergraduate students.

Upon the writing of this book, I have been in private practice in New York City for the better part of two decades providing therapy and also specialized private coaching. I am a clinical social worker licensed to provide therapy in New York, California, New Jersey, Pennsylvania, Illinois, Washington, D.C., and Massachusetts. In all other states and internationally I regularly work with people on a private coaching basis.

I do have several different specialties I work with aside from Grass Is Greener Syndrome including issues such as anxiety, depression, relationship issues, fear of flying, trauma therapy, panic attacks, and migraines. In my various areas of specialty, I have worked with numerous people who each have come with their own personal histories, experiences, and struggles. My interest as an integrative therapist is how to work with you personally based on the needs you have—emotionally, relationally, and psychologically—considering your own history, experiences, process, where you are now, and where you want to be.

For the sake of clarity, Grass Is Greener Syndrome is not a formal diagnosis. Its name is derived from a phrase that has been used casually over time to refer to the concept that there's something better elsewhere, which can only be found by abandoning the present and seeking a different reality. You might have heard someone say, "You know the grass isn't always greener on the other side," or something similar. This is often said about someone who is constantly looking elsewhere for the ideal situation (but also spoken by someone who knows that it's rarely so simple).

As I gained more experience in practice over time, I noticed a repetition with certain issues that I realized were not written about or even discussed anywhere. Frequently, people would either describe or display patterns of constantly looking for more and better, which seemed to be an endless search that was never fulfilled—whether finding relationships that at first seemed good, only to end them and start over after a period of time; or to have relocated geographically multiple times and still not be satisfied; or bouncing from one job or career to another out of repeated dissatisfaction. People would find themselves repeating these cycles again and again.

Many would be tortured by the fact that they couldn't settle down, or couldn't make a confident decision, especially with bigger life decisions. There would generally be a fantasy of another life path that would plague them, feeling torn between worlds, often not being able to understand which world made more sense to them or which to follow, and not knowing how to move forward or integrate them.

The more I saw these issues coming up, the more it became clear how common these patterns really are, and how misunderstood they were. The issues were clearly deeply entrenched, based on the repetitions of this cycle and the psychological, emotional, and relational patterns surrounding it. Even though each person didn't *want* to keep repeating the pattern, they couldn't help but repeat it anyway. This is where my interest in Grass Is Greener Syndrome started, and from there developed over time.

At this point, I have worked with many people who have reached out to me wanting to work through their grass is greener issues. Most come in feeling hopeless, helpless, and anxious, often having been through the cycle many times over before realizing something needed to be addressed that goes beyond the surface. If you're in this position, this book is a good start, but don't be afraid of getting help. Grass Is Greener Syndrome runs deep and is complex, and there's no shame in seeking help to overcome it, or for struggling with this issue in the first place. It is more common than you may realize.

How to Use This Book

In each chapter, you'll read about a different component of Grass Is Greener Syndrome that can often show up in one form or another. There will also be real life examples of different grass is greener struggles. Some of these examples may reflect your own struggle, or some may not, or only partially. Grass Is greener issues can show up differently for every person, as each person is coming from a different place internally and has had different life experiences.

Some concepts may be a bit confusing at times while other parts of the book you'll likely very much relate to and fully see yourself in.

It's okay if some parts don't completely make sense, or if you don't relate to everything in here. This book is meant to help you understand Grass Is Greener Syndrome and why it can have such a frustrating and debilitating hold over the trajectory of people's lives when they're entrenched in the cycle.

Hopefully, you will learn about yourself as you read along and start the process to overcoming this issue. However, this book isn't meant to cure Grass Is Greener Syndrome on its own, so don't expect everything to be fully resolved once you finish reading. Everything in this book is meant to help you start thinking about and getting to know your own struggle more in depth, and begin to reflect with curiosity so you can take the next step to move forward with your life. However your situation may be playing out in your life, there is help available for you.

Overall, if you feel that you struggle with grass is greener tendencies, or even if you don't but if you find yourself struggling with anything mentioned in this book, you're welcome to reach out and we can discuss how I can help you. My contact information is in the last page of this book.

CHAPTER 1

What Is Grass Is Greener Syndrome?

How often do you find yourself watching TV or ordering food from a restaurant and rather than simply committing to an option and enjoying the show or the meal, you instead find yourself thinking about the other options that might have been better? Maybe you're eating one meal and are now thinking you should have had that other one you almost chose instead. Or maybe you're watching a show that you enjoy, but now feel like you should have chosen the other one that you decided against. Or, maybe you're just scrolling through the other options, endlessly looking for the better show instead of really fully paying attention to the one you already chose.

Imagine going through this same kind of process, however, instead of TV or food, doing this in the most significant areas of your life. Repeatedly.

For anyone who struggles with Grass Is Greener Syndrome, they will tell you that it is one of the most conflicting, frustrating, and self-defeating struggles to endure. People who experience the ups and downs of this complicated and multifaceted issue can find it nearly impossible to settle down, and to *feel* settled in various areas of life. It can chronically feel like there is something better that you are missing out on. Almost like a magnified "fear of missing out" (FOMO) over the most significant parts of your life. In this case, it's not simply a worry of missing out on the party everyone else might be at, but more so a fear that you're possibly missing out on the better, or best, life.

In my practice, I have worked with people all over the world who struggle with Grass Is Greener Syndrome and related difficulties with commitment. Many people who struggle with Grass Is Greener Syndrome often don't realize it's playing out in their lives until the cycle becomes overpowering and all-consuming. It tends to wreak havoc on relationships, as well as the ability to maintain a career or jobs, or even where people may choose to live. It also often has a significant impact on decision-making in various ways in life. A grass is greener struggle generally sees people bouncing around, going from one situation or relationship to the next, chronically hoping the next one will ultimately both be better and feel better.

How Do You Experience Grass Is Greener Syndrome?
Throughout the course of this book, I will often reference the impact of Grass Is Greener Syndrome on relationships, mainly because relationships are the most common area this plays out. But if your grass is greener struggle plays out in another area of your life, just remember that anytime I mention relationships it can mean with people, but it can also mean relationships to your career, or where you live, or anything else. The greater issue is still the same cycle, either way.

Struggles with Grass Is Greener Syndrome in relationships can often lead to things such as infidelity, as well as relationship breakups, sometimes prematurely, or unnecessarily. When you experience grass is greener patterns, you may find you often struggle to feel connected and satisfied in your relationship. It is a common trait for people with Grass Is Greener Syndrome to have one foot out the door of their relationships, removing or at least distancing the ability to have intimacy, closeness, and fulfillment, which sets up an experience of distance to a relationship as a whole. It's very hard to fully feel a sense of satisfaction when one eye is still searching for the better option you may be missing.

If you're viewing it from the outside, Grass Is Greener Syndrome can be seen as a continuous cycle of seeking perfection. It is essentially a quest for the ideal—the ideal relationship, career, place to live, friendships, lifestyle, or otherwise. On the surface, it seems like a reasonable goal to find what fits your needs the most and set up your "best life." This isn't unreasonable, in and of itself.

However, the problem with Grass Is Greener Syndrome is that once you think you have found the ideal, the fulfillment is relatively short-lived. After the initial feeling of euphoria that comes with the newness of what seems like the ideal situation, the bright and fresh green grass slowly starts to fade. When this happens, it sparks what can feel like a constant internal tug-of-war that can't seem to be resolved. Almost as if you're finding yourself having to choose between either settling for less or having to start looking again for the shiny new ideal. Some impulsively jump to the next best-looking option, while others may become stuck in the indecision. Either of these are actually a part of the grass is greener struggle.

Difficulties with commitment and decision-making tend to be hallmarks of Grass Is Greener Syndrome. It can be terrifying to feel like you'll end up settling for less than what you need, or you may worry about settling into a potentially mundane life or relationship routine, or a kind of boredom where the passion for the relationship or life may end up dissipating over time.

Grass Is Greener Syndrome also often sees clashes of desire for closeness and intimacy, complicated by the deeper vulnerabilities and fears that can often limit this desired intimacy. The hardest part is that these struggles become circular in the grass is greener cycle. So, it isn't only one decision to break up, or to stay, or otherwise that must be made. These feelings and fears tend to show up again and again, in whatever the current situation may be.

The Starvation of Needs

How long can you go without food before you're starving and know you *need* to eat? Everyone has emotional states of being. You may feel happy, sad, disappointed, anxious, fulfilled, joyful, grief, and so on. Your emotional states are always where they are at any point in time based on a number of factors in your internal and external environment. Right now, in the various areas of your life, your emotions—or sense of satisfaction, fulfillment, or dissatisfaction—are responding to what you are, and aren't, receiving. Some needs are being nourished, even unconsciously behind the scenes without you fully being aware of it, while others are being less nourished or not nourished at all.

When you're caught in the grass is greener cycle, it is common to experience a split between feelings of fulfillment and of deprivation in the part of your life that's in conflict. For example, maybe you're missing the passion you crave, or the intimacy, sex, excitement, joy, mental stimulation, or any other wishes for fulfillment that haven't been there recently. When this starts to happen, it can become almost automatic for your focus to become consumed by what's missing. You start to feel so deprived of certain needs that you may almost completely be unable to see or experience the parts that are more fulfilled. If you're starving, it's hard to think of anything else until the starvation is nourished.

Looking at relationships, for example, you may have certain desires and needs that are being fulfilled by your current relationship. Because these are qualities you've largely become accustomed to in the day-to-day of your relationship, you may not consciously notice them anymore. These unconscious need fulfillments are the qualities that support the relationship—often comprised by the "little things," but can also include larger-scale needs as well. For some, these can be things like trust, care, reliability, partnership, respect, consistency, and more.

While the fulfillment of these needs plays out in the background, the routine nature of them being there makes them less conscious and less noticeable. You're not hungry or starving for them, because they're at least somewhat routinely being fed. As a result, a person with Grass Is Greener Syndrome will start to become more consciously aware of what qualities the relationship is lacking—where you are becoming hungrier. And these missing qualities become the focus because these are the needs that are being starved out. You notice what is *missing* from your relationship more than you are able to notice what *supports* the relationship because when a need is starving, its cry is louder.

As more time goes by and your craving continues to grow for the needs you're missing, it eventually feels like you're completely starving and can no longer tolerate the void. This often includes but is not exclusive to things like sex, affection, love, care, passion, attention, appreciation, excitement, and anything else you need to have in a relationship. The more starved the needs are, the more this becomes the preoccupation.

In response to this, you may start to unintentionally (or intentionally) look around for someone else who can meet those starved needs, whether through cheating, an affair, or breaking up and starting over altogether. Or, you may start looking for your next job or career, or where you're going to move to next. The overall hope is that you'll nourish what's missing and then you'll no longer feel deprived or so deeply in need. The fantasy becomes that the new situation is going to fulfill the starved need and complete the picture of what you're missing. Everything will hopefully then be fulfilled, and you'll be happy and satisfied in your life. The quest for the ideal relationship will be complete once you find someone (or situation) who can fill all of these starved needs for you.

However, what people in the grass is greener cycle tend to overlook is that in order to go to the new environment to fill the voids, your total emotional environment is going to change with that. Rather than simply adding the missing pieces to the picture, a major change, like a relationship breakup, is going to change the picture altogether. With this change inevitably comes losing pieces that were also unknowingly being nurtured in the previous space.

Therefore, when you start over, you're not actually *completing* your present emotional environment as much as just making it different. Maybe it will be better, maybe it won't. But the idea that you're just going to complete what's missing is somewhat of a fallacy that is often misunderstood. In starting over, people often find they've fed the starved needs, as desired, but in the process they end up now with new sets of unmet needs that slowly start to starve. This ends up reinforcing the grass is greener cycle.

This is the driving narrative of Grass Is Greener Syndrome—the "next one" will be the ideal one. The next one will be the one you've been looking for all along. It will resolve all of the disappointments and deprivations, and the grass will finally stay bright green once you've found it. If only it were so simple, then Grass Is Greener Syndrome wouldn't be a thing.

Not Better, Just Different

What usually ends up happening in Grass Is Greener Syndrome is you may find someone with those qualities you've been missing, jump into that relationship, and feel immediately gratified. In the moment, it is the biggest feeling of relief. And it often feels euphoric, like a high—at least for a bit of time. However, eventually you may start realizing that you're now missing the good qualities of either the previous relationship, or you may begin yearning for an entirely different relationship, again.

But why? Didn't you finally just find everything you needed?

The answer is: Yes. You found exactly what you needed in order to nourish yourself when you were starving. However, as part of this, you've actually left certain qualities behind that were unconsciously fulfilling other needs—qualities that support the relationship. These were the background needs that were unconsciously being fulfilled on a routine basis. You've now left those behind in order to nourish the starved needs. In the most basic terms, you've ended up unintentionally trading one set of needs for another.

At first, in the new situation, you were previously so starved from the deprivation of what you've been missing that all you feel is euphoria and relief. As if everything you've ever needed is finally right here, and this is everything you've been missing and craving. It feels like there is no place you'd rather be than where you are now and your search is done. Which seems ideal. That is, until you start to notice that a new set of needs is now missing from the new relationship picture. As time passes, you slowly become starved and deprived all over again (of similar or different needs than before). And, thus, the grass is greener cycle repeats.

It's worth mentioning that it can be very difficult when in a state of almost total starvation to choose a relationship based on anything more than pure need fulfillment. Again, when you're starving you need to eat. At this point, it becomes a change nearly on impulse. This unfortunately only propels the grass is greener cycle forward, as the next repetition is often actually being set up right from the start.

Whenever you switch from one relationship to another, you are going to gain and lose elements. There will be pros and cons. You're not just going to add without subtracting. You may gain the excitement, the spontaneity, the sex, the adventure, the passion, but you may, for example, lose the reliability, trust, consistency, safety, and more. It's very hard when within the grass is greener cycle to internalize that a new relationship is going to be *different*, but not necessarily better or worse than the previous one. The needs will be different, the fulfillments will be different, the pros and cons will be different. But either way, if you're in the grass is greener cycle, it's likely that something at some point will starve.

You've probably heard the saying, "Wherever you go, there you are." This is relevant with Grass Is Greener Syndrome. Not only do the grass is greener patterns come with you to the next, but any other psychological, emotional, and relational patterns that are carried in your life also come with you from one environment to the next. If you don't address the things you bring with you, they'll find a way to show up again, even if the change brings a temporary reprieve.

A NOTE ON THE EXAMPLES

When reading the examples, it's important to keep in mind that we're looking at the grass is greener mindset. This means that in some instances, we'll only be looking at one side of a relationship without going into what issues the other person brings to the table that may also be impacting the relationship. This isn't to say there aren't other or more dynamics at play, or that both people don't contribute to the issues. But more to be aware that when we're looking at relationships that the person struggling with grass is greener issues isn't automatically a villain and the other a victim.

The hope is to relay how the grass is greener struggles ultimately makes it more difficult to recover from issues that arise. The focus when reading the examples is how, when you're in the grass is greener cycle, the problems that arise tend to trigger reactions that lead to patterns of more distance and ambivalence in the relationship, which, if not addressed, often leads to starting over.

Each example focuses on one piece of Grass Is Greener Syndrome that's covered in the corresponding chapter (except for Ariana's in Chapter 8, which combines several of the grass is greener traits together). Generally speaking, when people struggle with Grass Is Greener Syndrome it's usually a collection of symptoms and elements happening together. Therefore, you may recognize yourself in several stories, but you may not recognize yourself in all of them since not everyone struggles with every area of Grass Is Greener Syndrome.

In each example, all identifying information and details have been changed and restructured to not represent any one specific person who I've worked with. Confidentiality is something I care greatly about and is fully protected. If we have worked together and you believe you recognize yourself in any of the stories, rest assured that none of the stories are attributed to any one person, and each story is essentially a picture created by pieces fit together from many different puzzles.

STORY #1: AMY

Amy was thirty years old when she started working on her grass is greener patterns. She had been looking for a relationship that she could settle down in long-term. She wanted to get married and eventually have kids, but had been struggling to find a partner who felt like a good match for her. Amy had had relationships on and off since high school—she was no stranger to them. However, all of her relationships had lasted for less than three years, the longest of which was her first one after college.

Amy knew she needed help when she noticed each of her relationships ended because she couldn't maintain a sense of fulfillment. In all of them except for one, she broke up with her partners because she didn't feel like the relationships were able to satisfy what she needed. The one time she was broken up with was because she became so distant and checked out that her partner at the time ended it.

Amy noticed that no matter what the issue would be each time around, the relationship would never be enough to sustain the level of stimulation and fulfillment she wanted. Disappointment always came up, even after the relationships were so promising at the beginning. At first she would be all in, craving time and closeness with whichever guy she was dating. She would have no doubt that the relationship was right for her.

However, eventually Amy would struggle with her level of commitment as the relationship moved forward. It generally would get to a point where she'd have one foot out the door and begin unconsciously looking around at other possibilities. To her, it felt like if she wanted to get married and have kids, then the partner she chose to settle down with must really be no less than the "right" or "best" one. This is a reasonable desire, of course, but the search was proving to be chronically frustrating, always coming up short. While she knew many people truly weren't good enough and she shouldn't settle for less, she also suspected there was something going on with the stuff she was bringing into her relationships that was making things harder for her to find the results she wanted.

One of her relationships ended because she wanted to actively do more fun things—like hiking together, taking small trips, or doing other activities—and she didn't feel like her partner was as active or desired the same level of activity, which left her feeling bored and alone. Another ended because she felt like the level of intimacy she desired wasn't met. While her partner was steady and reliable, their sex life was underwhelming and she felt generally like she was missing passion in her life as a whole, which she felt was exacerbated by her relationship.

Whatever the needs would be in each relationship, it seemed like Amy was always starving from some iteration of boredom and under-whelm. She could only seem to achieve the level of fulfillment and excitement she wanted when in a new relationship. However, simply knowing this about herself wasn't enough to stop her from repeatedly ending relationships and starting over with the hope that the next person would be the one to sustain the excitement and level of stimu-lation she wanted.

In each relationship, the feeling that she wasn't getting enough stim-ulation and connection would grow slowly until eventually this feeling of starvation became so strong that she needed to fulfill it. Amy thought she would lose hope and fall into a depression if she didn't pursue this need outside of the relationship. This yearning would ultimately lead her to break up with whichever boyfriend she was with at the time in order to pursue the hope of the next one. A couple of times, she had already started to see another man while she was still with her current boyfriend.

It was only once she was out of her relationship and dating some-one new that Amy felt like she finally had everything she was looking for. This was the only point in time she consistently felt like she was no longer starving. However, she would eventually notice the feeling slowly returning. This would usually happen once the relationship settled into a routine and daily life started to play more of a role. Sometimes it was a repetitious feeling of boredom; sometimes the starvation would come from lack of emotional intimacy. Or she would be with someone who wasn't as reliable or predictable and it would feel like she needed the reliability back in order to make her less anxious in the relationship. There was always a new point of starvation that would make her seek out another relationship. Once she realized this, she knew something needed to change if she wanted to have a successful and fulfilling long-term relationship.

While the overall foundation of her grass is greener issues were more complex, it turns out that Amy grew up in a house where everybody (parents and siblings) were all motivated by achieving. If she was wasting time, doing nothing, or not being productive, it always felt like she wasn't doing enough, or that she was going to fail. This frame of mind was a significant contributor to her overall grass is greener mentality (there was also more complexity from other grass is greener elements described in the next chapters). If there were lulls, it felt like the relationship couldn't be enough to nurture her and would fall apart. To mitigate this, she would leave the relationship and find a new one to nourish her needs before the current one could hurt her or fail.

After spending time working through the patterns that were holding her back, Amy has now been in a relationship for seven years that she feels fulfilled and empowered in. In the past, when a lull would happen, she would lose confidence in the relationship and leave. She is now able to approach the lulls with a different perspective and confidence in her relationship.

CHAPTER 2

The Foundation of Grass Is Greener Syndrome

If the starvation of needs was the entirety of the issue, overcoming Grass Is Greener Syndrome wouldn't be as complicated. What makes Grass Is Greener Syndrome so tough is the fact that it is the result of a collection of psychological, emotional, and relational experiences that are constantly working together to challenge the foundation of connection, commitment, and intimacy.

Grass Is Greener Syndrome isn't your regular everyday commitment or decision-making issue. Difficulty with commitment is one symptom of the larger issue, but someone who struggles with commitment may or may not have a grass is greener issue. The same goes for decision-making. Both commitment and decision-making are problems within Grass Is Greener Syndrome, which often becomes more and more difficult as grass is greener patterns are repeatedly reinforced. Every time you start over and it doesn't work out as hoped, the cycle strengthens. It can become difficult to continue trusting your own decisions when seeing that they repeatedly are not working out in your favor.

The reality is, by the time you start actively experiencing and becoming consciously aware of grass is greener patterns playing out in all of its self-sabotaging glory, the foundation has likely already been strongly built beneath the surface psychologically, emotionally, and relationally.

Perfectionism

People who struggle with perfectionism will tell you that it both drives and helps them at times but can also really get in their way and cause a lot more stress and anxiety than they'd like. With perfectionism, less than perfect isn't good enough. It is either perfection, or failure.

Grass Is Greener Syndrome often involves a battle with perfectionism. When in the grass is greener cycle, the search to find the "right," "best," or "perfect" fit in one area or another is very common. There is often an image in mind, whether consciously or unconsciously, of how the perfect image should look and feel, and what needs should be met when you've found it. If there's not a full visual image consciously in mind, then there is generally at the least an expectation of what the feeling or experience should be like when you've found what you're looking for.

This, unfortunately, is one of the most reinforcing parts of Grass Is Greener Syndrome. Perfectionism is rooted in the concept of getting the situation exactly "right." While it's good and healthy to have an understood set of standards and desires for yourself, crossing into the area of perfectionism can often backfire.

Perfectionism is an all-or-nothing process. You either keep going until you've perfected the picture, or it's not good enough. Without achieving perfection, you feel you haven't succeeded yet, and thus anything less than perfect will be experienced as a form of disappointment or failure.

What's difficult about perfectionism with Grass Is Greener Syndrome is that at first, in the honeymoon phase, it may feel like you've found the perfect match. However, once that shiny new green grass starts to wear off, it suddenly feels like you've lost the perfection. It can be really difficult for many to know how to find fulfillment in the grey areas if less than perfect. How can a person feel happy and fulfilled in a relationship where there is also disappointment and lack of fulfillment, at times? When it's difficult to know how to be in the middle ground, losing the certainty and the perfection flips from fulfillment to a feeling of uncertain and not good enough. It leads to retreating from a relationship, feeling doubtful, pulling mentally and emotionally away, and starting to wonder what else is out there that will be perfect.

Perfectionism, whether in a grass is greener cycle or on its own, is often a self-defeating and self-sabotaging process. As long as you're able to maintain the perfection, then things are okay. However, once you start to come into contact with imperfections (which is inevitable when spending enough time with anyone or anything), in an all-or-nothing process the feeling quickly can go from perfection to doubtful.

With Grass Is Greener Syndrome you're either existing in the perfection and euphoria of the shiny new phase, or you're feeling unfulfilled by something that used to be more ideal at the start and is no longer good enough. There is very little middle ground in grass is greener processes and people can spend their whole lives bouncing back and forth trying to find everlasting perfection.

Expectations
It's normal to have expectations. Everybody has them to some degree. They're useful to help us build the kind of life we want to have. However, similar to perfectionism, when the expectations exceed a certain threshold, they can also backfire.

High expectations are another driver of the grass is greener cycle. Expectations are formed throughout childhood, growing up and interacting with the world around you, which involves a variety of situations you see and experience every day (even including made-up scenarios such as stories created for movies and TV, for example). Sometimes, it can be complicated to understand where expectations are reasonable and where they are possibly standing in our own way more than helping us. When are we chasing something reasonably attainable, and when are we chasing something theoretically attainable, but also reasonably unrealistic?

This window of uncertainty sets up an internal conflict about which competing voices you should be listening to. Do you keep searching to match your expectations fully, or are certain expectations perpetuating the repetition? Would it help to compromise and learn to manage certain expectations that are making things harder? For many, this can feel like a frustrating and intolerable request. Why should you have to settle for less than you want or need? When the answer between these voices isn't clear, it can be very difficult to know what to do.

This internal conflict is a significant driver in Grass Is Greener Syndrome. It's one thing to *know* consciously that certain expectations or needs are making some things more difficult for you; it's another thing to *emotionally* understand this and be emotionally able to modify or compromise certain needs.

For example, let's say you need to have the honeymoon phase version of feeling in love at all times in order to feel satisfied in your relationship. If you get to a point where you don't experience the in-love feelings on a somewhat regular basis, you may struggle to understand if this means you're in the wrong relationship (since that feeling didn't last), or if this is just too high of an expectation.

If at some point you come to realize it may be too much to expect that in-love euphoria to be there all the time, you may understand it consciously, but that's not going to stop you from having a strong need to fill the void emotionally. It will feel like something is missing that is a strong area of emotional need. It's one thing to have a realization in thought, it's another to bring your emotions to align with that realization.

Projection

Projection is defense mechanism that happens unconsciously when owning a certain aspect of ourselves consciously would be too big of a threat for the ego to tolerate. For example, we may not want to acknowledge the parts of ourselves that can sometimes be selfish or self-serving (especially if you are bothered by people who display these qualities). Acknowledging them may be potentially damaging to one's ego, whether because there is something about these particular qualities, or perhaps simply any quality that makes a person view themselves as flawed or imperfect.

As a result, on a deeper subconscious level we avoid acknowledging that we can be self-serving at times, and instead we become frustrated (often on an amplified level) when we experience someone else's selfish parts. In projection, it's easier and safer to vilify someone else's selfishness rather than to acknowledge and accept our own.

This is just one example of projection. The general idea with projection is that we place an experience of our own imperfection outside of ourselves and onto others (even if it may not even be accurate about the other person). We do this unconsciously, not purposefully, in protection of our own ego.

So how does this impact Grass Is Greener Syndrome? Grass Is Greener Syndrome in some ways is a multilayered projection of perfectionism. We project our own imperfections outward, away from ourselves, in order to gratify the deeper wish to find perfection in ourselves. This happens when our ego hasn't yet built the fortitude to tolerate our own imperfections, insecurities, and shame. This involves an acting out of our own desire for perfection. Or, in simpler terms, we keep searching for perfection in the world when we can't tolerate our own imperfections. If we can merge with perfection, then we can see ourselves as perfect.

Since we as human beings can't actually be flawless, perfectionism (and the projection of it) is like fighting a battle that you can never quite win—which is the never-ending grass is greener cycle.

As long as we remain dissociated from our own imperfections, the moment we start to see imperfections outside of ourselves, we can't tolerate it. We instead may criticize it, or try to perfect it, or find another more perfect option instead. The inability to sit with our own imperfections makes the grass fade when we start to see other's imperfections, especially when we're projecting our wish for perfection onto them. Once we start to see the imperfections in the other it may feel intolerable and disappointing, and maybe even disillusioning (since our own imperfections may be). Rather than flaws being normal and okay, if we can't tolerate them in ourselves then we can't tolerate it outside of ourselves, either.

Some might say, "Well, I know I'm not perfect, I just want someone who is better than me." And others might say, "If I can find someone who is perfect, then it shows me I can be, too." Either way is the same losing battle. Both involves the same disavowing of one's own flaws for the other who can cover for what the ego may not yet be ready to tolerate. The first one is a self-defeating double standard that essentially says, "I'm not perfect, but you have to be," and the second says that no imperfections are allowed at all.

STORY #2: STEVE

Steve is forty-eight-years old and has always had an interest in dating different women. In college for all of his twenties, he struggled to maintain a relationship because he always wanted to keep his options open. He always felt that there were others who would be better, and it resulted in short-term relationships that he would end once he started to sense that whoever he was dating in the moment wanted more commitment from him (they would also at times leave him first due to his lack of commitment).

In Steve's relationships, there would often come a make-or-break point where he had to either decide to continue the relationship and put both feet in the door, or he had to move on. Steve feared two things: One was that he was always missing out on someone better who he would eventually settle down with (which was a never-ending search); and the other was a fear of getting into a relationship and finding that he couldn't do it. The guilt he would face if he committed and then betrayed his partner was something that prevented him from taking the next step every time it was possible.

This combination—the fear of failure, causing pain to his partner by leaving, and always feeling there was a better option—led to him constantly leaving relationships before they really had a solid chance to succeed. As a result, Steve would keep relationships at arm's length, effectively not allowing anything to ever deepen or grow beyond a certain point.

With each relationship, there was always something missing. He didn't have a clear sense of what his expectations fully were, but Steve just knew there was always something he wasn't getting that would feel right when he got it. He believed that if he found the perfect woman, then he would never feel the yearning for another one. This would be the sign of happiness and finding "the one." Therefore, every time he was in a relationship and felt his attention pulled to another woman, he took it to mean that he should still be looking. According to Steve, if another woman got his attention, then clearly there was still better out there.

Steve met a woman when he was thirty-one who he'd eventually go on to marry. She seemed to have everything he was looking for, however, there was always some sort of doubt that lingered. As good as the relationship was, he couldn't sustain a feeling of fulfillment. But he knew that the relationship was the best he had found to this point, and he knew he wanted to settle down, so he married her. They eventually had two kids. By this point, they had been together for eight years.

Underneath, though, Steve couldn't shake the idea that there was someone perfect who would bring fulfillment more easily. He struggled with the expectations that somebody perfect existed and felt he just needed to find this person who would make life feel easy for him.

Eventually, Steve ended up having an affair, and ultimately decided that he needed to break off the marriage to pursue a relationship with this other woman. According to Steve, this time he had found the perfect woman who seemed to meet all of his expectations of what relationships should feel and be like. There was a constant passion and craving for each other that seemed so euphoric and satisfying. They wanted to take care of each other. And they aligned in various other ways in terms of interests. This felt different and more exciting than the relationship with his wife.

After about nine months in this new relationship, things began to shift. Steve noticed that the feeling wasn't the same anymore. He remembered this feeling because it scared him when he previously first felt it with his wife. This was the feeling that maybe she wasn't perfect after all. These same doubts were returning now, and he found himself starting to regret his divorce.

This is when Steve realized that if he didn't address this pattern then it would likely endlessly continue to hurt all of his relationships. He started to recall that the same sense of excitement and care was also there with his wife at first, too—that it wasn't really different with the new relationship that he left his family for. Except now he was riddled with guilt and regret for leaving his family and yearned to return. The grass wasn't greener in the new relationship, and now the greener grass seemed to be the relationship he'd already left.

Over time, Steve worked on understanding the level of expectations he has unconsciously set in his relationships, the amount of pressure for perfection he puts onto a relationship, and how he projects this need for perfection onto women as a means to take away his own fears of inadequacy that have always plagued him deeper down in his life. He wasn't able to return to his marriage. However, as he's worked through the foundation of his grass is greener tendencies and his own lifelong battle with insecurity, he's found himself able to sustain fulfillment in his current relationship and able to navigate disappointments that show up without feeling the need to run to the next.

CHAPTER 3

The Grass Is Greener Cycle

It is often difficult for people to tell the difference between "commitment issues" versus a greater grass is greener pattern. To be fair, commitment struggles are one significant piece of the grass is greener process. However, there is a difference between a struggle to commit and a greater process of self-sabotage that can play out. Grass Is Greener Syndrome tends to have a general cycle to it: idealization (honeymoon), disappointment, disillusionment, devaluation, and then starting over and repetition of the cycle.

I'm presenting this cycle with idealization first since it's a bit easier to see it starting when things are good—when the grass is greenest—and then when they change. However, I consider the grass is greener cycle to really begin with the disappointment phase. This is when something happens that stirs a sense of internal conflict, and starts the feeling of deprivation. This is where the struggle starts. Some might say that starting over into idealization is more of a reprieve from the conflict cycle. However, it is still part of the cycle, in a sort of similar way that an abuse cycle often has a reconciliation/honeymoon phase after an incident. There may not be abuse occurring in a phase where things are good, but it still feeds and is part of the overall system. The good phases are in many ways what propels the repetition of the cycle forward, even if the turmoil starts in the disappointment phase.

You're the Greatest—Idealization

Idealization is a process that originates as a child, where we look up to our parents as the ideal representatives of the world. It is a normal process for someone to go through a phase (or phases) of idealization. This tends to be something that shows up when someone else has what we ourselves are craving or needing, which starts with the relationship to our parents as infants. It is a feeling of the other person being "perfect." As people, we look up to this "ideal" person as a model to follow in the world for who we want to be or who we need to learn from in order to shape ourselves into who we'd ideally like to be.

Idealization is also common early on in a relationship. In a phase of idealization, the experience is usually a euphoric feeling. You've found everything you've ever wanted—it feels like perfection. Your life, on the inside and outside, feels like it's solved, and now you are happy and complete. You've found the perfect person, and you feel fantastic. It seems that nothing, or no one, can really be better. This is the phase that has received the label "the honeymoon phase" with respect to relationships. It also is what tends to be referred to as "infatuation" due to this feeling often coming before relationships have had the opportunity to develop more depth and growth. However, when in a phase of idealization, it can feel so euphoric that people tend to experience it as being "in love." (We'll save the philosophical discussions of what defines "love" or "not love" for another time).

On a rational level, people often realize that the idealization phase can only go so far before other non-ideal day-to-day life stuff, or human imperfection, becomes part of the relationship and one person (or both) emerges from the safe cocoon of idealization. However, on an emotional level, the idealization and euphoria tends to feel so powerfully validating that the expectation and hope is that it will never go away. When idealization does start to falter, it can set off profound feelings of loss, disappointment, anger, grief, and other feelings of being let down and disoriented. The desire is for the relationship to stay ideal, or very close to there.

For people who tend to struggle most with grass is greener issues, the problem isn't only a wish for this ideal phase to stick around; the problem is that idealization often serves as the criteria on which people base the legitimacy of their relationship. That *this* is what the "right" relationship looks like, or what love is supposed to be and feels like. Therefore, if you lose this feeling, then the worry becomes that it must not be the relationship you're looking for, and must not be the best relationship you can find.

Maybe Not the Greatest—Disappointment

If you're reading this, I imagine at some point in the course of your life you've experienced the feeling of disappointment. For some, disappointment can be a tolerable even if unwelcome feeling. For others, disappointment can be a really complicated feeling. It is difficult to emphasize just how deep the feeling of disappointment can run, and the amount of unconscious self-destructive and self-sabotaging tendencies that chronic disappointment can actually cause as people try to defend against potential disappointment.

When a person is chronically disappointed, either from their own expectations of the world or by others who simply aren't able to meet their expectations, they can often start acting in preparation for disappointment by creating self-fulfilling prophecies—meaning they can unconsciously set up the exact disappointment or pain that they are wanting to prevent. This can show up in many forms and for different reasons. While many hope that being prepared for disappointment can make it feel less painful when disappointment happens, preparing for disappointment can actually serve to create it.

For example, you might find ways push your partner away in order to test the strength of your relationship (this can happen consciously or unconsciously). As a result, all you really end up doing is pushing your partner away to a distance in the relationship. Your partner becomes more reluctant to come close now, and then you end up disappointed that the intimacy is lacking. Self-sabotage and self-fulfilling prophecies are commonly played out by people who struggle with chronic disappointment.

However, an important point for the sake of this discussion is that when someone is chronically disappointed as a person and then becomes disappointed in the relationship, it starts an internal crisis and panic. Maybe the relationship is wrong, maybe the person is bad, maybe they made a mistake, and so on. As a result of this crisis, a guard can be put up, which includes taking one foot out of the door of the relationship. It may feel self-protective in response to a history of disappointment and hurt. However, this ends up having an impact on the relationship as a whole.

Keep in mind that if someone has the "perfect" relationship, then it's not supposed to be disappointing. This disappointment happening at all, on some level, automatically means to the perfectionist that this isn't the right person. If they are no longer ideal, then the idealization didn't last, and therefore it must mean that the relationship isn't the right one.

Now, to be clear, the first disappointment doesn't always cause this cascade to happen. At first it may just be a bit unsettling to see that the person *can* be disappointing at all. But then after enough disappointments, that's when the panic starts.

Who Is This Person?—Disillusionment
The difference between disappointment and disillusionment is somewhat subtle but important. Disappointment is a feeling of being let

down—when something doesn't go the way you hoped or when you expected better from someone or something only to come up short.

Disillusionment goes a step beyond this. Disillusionment is the breaking of the idealization. This is the realization, or enlightenment—whether on a deeper or more surface level—that this person (or place, etc.) is not what you thought after all. The illusion is no longer able to be sustained. Either enough disappointments or the type of disappointment has made it clear that who you idealized at first isn't the same person as you held in that perfect image. This often happens when we as human beings start to see that our parents are also "just" human beings as well. It isn't simply that "the honeymoon" is over as much as it goes from the person you thought could give you everything you've ever been missing to just being another flawed person.

With disillusionment generally comes a sense of disorientation since it can often feel like you're seeing a person for the first time in certain ways, or that you aren't sure who they are anymore. It's still the same person, but there are sides to them that you may not have fully come into contact with yet. So when you "meet" a new side of someone and it creates disillusionment, this also brings disorientation of where you are in relation to this person, and where you stand in the relationship. There's almost a sense of before and after that comes with disillusionment.

This brings such a sense of conflict because it can feel like you were being fooled. Disillusionment can often bring anger and shame with it—anger for being fooled, and shame for ever allowing yourself to feel so close, safe, and vulnerable with just another flawed person. This combination of anger and shame can lead you to project blame onto the other person for ever allowing you to feel so safe—almost as if you were fooled because the other person was hiding their bad parts that would have saved you from vulnerability. This leads to the next phase of the cycle.

Not Good Enough—Devaluation

Devaluation tends to follow when the disorientation that happens from the disillusionment cannot be processed or integrated. Many haven't had the appropriate role modeling, guidance, or experience to know how to hold, process, or integrate these moments without having to blow everything up in response. Disorientation can be quite unsettling, but it doesn't have to lead to leaving or starting over. However, in the perfectionistic grass is greener process, it is very hard to hold the other's disillusioning flaws along with the idea of integrating them. The other person is no longer perfect (and, therefore, neither is the relationship), so "what's the point in trying" is generally the feeling.

The experiences of disappointment and disillusionment can be incredibly, deeply painful. The desire to run away as a reaction usually tends to be out of fear. It's really scary for people to believe that there's only so close to perfect or ideal that a person or relationship can really be. Where there is a deep void or starvation you're experiencing, or there are needs that are not being fulfilled, it can feel hopeless and earth-shattering to imagine that accepting a "good enough" relationship can *actually* be good enough. When it's hard to find or emotionally experience the middle ground between perfect and not good enough, good enough doesn't exist. Good enough just sounds like settling for less. It's only "not good enough." In these instances, if the depth of the void is too great or your needs aren't being fully met, then it feels like you're just going to spend life living in disappointment and deprivation.

This leads to devaluation. This is a combination of shame and anger that comes from allowing yourself to be vulnerable to a flawed person, and the feeling that not only is the relationship not the ideal you once thought (and felt) it was, but now you have the conviction that it's actually wrong and not good enough, or even bad. You may have turned to feelings of hate for the partner (the all-or-nothing flip), or feel complete disgust and anger at the relationship and/or towards yourself for ever thinking this relationship could have been right in the first place.

Devaluing is simply a state of feeling the same person who was everything and ideal is no longer good enough or worth it. You were wrong about them and they're not worth the time, your emotion, your vulnerability, or anything else. The drop from perfect to not good enough is the devaluation. This is where the grass is greener cycle starts to flip back towards starting over if there isn't an effort made to resolve the disillusionment. At this point in the cycle, the void is likely becoming more and more consuming over the relationship since you're being starved of all the perfections and ideals that this person previously filled. You're now not only one foot in and one foot out, but in many cases both feet may be out the door, just searching for the next relationship to bring you back to idealization and feeding those starved needs again.

Time to Try Again—Starting Over

The ending and starting over phase isn't really a phase. It's simply the action of choosing to start over. Once people who struggle with Grass Is Greener Syndrome fall into the devaluation phase, leaving and starting over can be almost inevitable if they're not consciously recognizing the pattern taking place and wanting to work on it.

Prior to reaching the decision to start over, many try to resolve the issue in their mind first. It may seem that it all happens very quickly and impulsively, but there can actually be a significant amount of time spent in each phase where things slowly shift, and they can also quickly shift as well. But when you don't have the appropriate role modeling or experiences to handle this cycle, thought processes usually fall into the self-sabotage or self-fulfilling prophecy mode at this point because you've already been disillusioned and hurt and the guards are going up. It's going to be easier to find ways to keep the distance than it's going to be to get too close again.

In this phase, you may try to think yourself away from the bad, but without being able to resolve the fact that human flaws and disappointments exist, even in the best relationships, it likely becomes a futile rumination more than a productive exercise. All of this tends to happen while one or likely both feet are already out the door after reaching devaluation. Once you are starving and can't find a way to refill the void with the same person (and other outside options therefore become the greenest grass), this is when people generally leave the relationship and start over.

STORY #3: MELANIE

Melanie is twenty-seven years old. When she was twenty-two, Melanie started therapy for anxiety related to adjusting out of college and for bouts of depression that were also happening at the time. As things in her life moved forward post-college, the focus in her therapy turned to issues with her relationships, and a noticeable grass is greener pattern started to emerge.

When she was in her last year of college, Melanie began to date Sam, who was a year older than her and had already graduated college. When she first met Sam, he was the ideal image of what she felt a relationship should be. He had a career he was starting to build, he was responsible, he took care of himself financially, and he had a wide circle of friends he would spend time with regularly. He was attentive to her and supportive of her interests and the things she was doing in her life. They both would enjoy activities together, and would also enjoy just being together, even if they didn't always go out. They would sometimes just spend the weekend lying in bed, watching movies, and having sex.

While she knew it was "too soon" to say she loved him after a couple of months, it was clear Melanie saw Sam as the ideal. The world felt right to Melanie now that Sam was in it. They would text constantly, and she noted that she would blush when she would receive an unexpected text from him. This all reflected to her that the relationship was "right."

After about five months into the relationship—after Melanie had finished college and was now working a full-time job while also living alone outside of college for the first time—the tone seemed to change a bit. Sam apparently had some habits that were becoming a turnoff to Melanie. He sometimes wouldn't respond to texts for hours, even when she knew he likely had time because he used to always respond within twenty to thirty minutes. He would also now make plans with his friends on nights they could have spent together, which was becoming more limited now that she would sometimes have to work on Saturdays (when she didn't have to before she graduated).

Melanie noticed that Sam wasn't making the same efforts to be there with her and be supportive to her anymore as well. She began to feel deprioritized and disappointed, but it was an issue that they were able to work through over time, even if the idealization had been dented. For Melanie, these disappointments were real but manageable. And they didn't lead to a greater grass is greener cascade.

A few months after this—about a year into their relationship now—Melanie ended up with a significant opportunity in the career she was building. As part of this opportunity, she was going to earn a higher salary than Sam, and it was putting her closer to her own career goals than Sam was to his. He responded to her opportunity with an argument that essentially tried to talk her out of taking the position. In this argument, Melanie was introduced to a side of Sam that she hadn't seen before. It was very different than the supportive and affectionate partner who would celebrate her and her accomplishments. It suddenly felt like they were in competition with each other, with Sam seeming to be threatened by her success.

As a result of this, Melanie started to become disillusioned with Sam and the overall relationship. Though her upset and disappointment were valid, this changed both her view of Sam and her experience of the relationship. It was disorienting and it became difficult to reconcile this unsupportive and competitive side of Sam with the one she had come to see earlier on as the perfect partner. For the first time, it felt like she really didn't know who Sam was and wasn't sure if she should be dating him. She began to distance herself and effectively (and unconsciously) put one foot out the door. She wondered if all relationships were like this or if there was better that she was missing out on.

Prior to this argument, there had been talk of moving in together in another six months or so. However, once this disillusionment set in, she began to wonder if she could continue to date him at all. Sam eventually recognized how he hurt Melanie and tried to apologize. But at this point, Melanie was struggling to reconcile the disillusionment. Sam had become just another flawed and insecure man who she felt would always prioritize himself and his goals over hers and try to stifle her success.

She started to feel disgusted with Sam and also with herself for ever becoming vulnerable to him in the first place, realizing that she didn't "really" know who he was. She became preoccupied with Sam's negative qualities to a point that she could no longer see him as someone loveable to her, and could now barely recall what she ever saw in him. She noticed herself wanting more and more distance, even when he would try to make time for her. Eventually, she decided that if she's feeling this way in the relationship that she knew there would be better for her out there, so she broke up with Sam. This was about a year and a half into their relationship (which would have coincided with when they were talking about moving in together).

It's important to point out here that Melanie's example is less about understanding if they were well matched or who was bringing more challenging stuff to the relationship. The greater issue of the cycle is what's necessary to notice. For Melanie, her relationships generally went in this cycle. Once she started to come into contact with her partner's flaws, it pushed her to distance, partially out the door, and to a place of the relationship not being "good enough." It would become a cascade that became difficult to stop from overpowering her. This repeated prior to Sam in three other relationships. And it started to repeat in her next relationship as well. However, this time the pattern was something she was able to address in her therapy as it started to play out again and she was becoming more acquainted with her tendencies in relationships. Through the process of her work, Melanie has been more able to catch the cascade and effectively work through disappointment and disillusionment without them consuming her. This has helped her to break the overall cycle, allowing her to take control of it rather than the cycle controlling her.

CHAPTER 4

Emotional Deprivation

It is doubtful you will encounter a human being who has not felt the pain of deprivation at some point over the course of their lives. Some people have had to learn to live with deprivation whether they want to or not. No matter the reason, emotional deprivation brings a deeper pain that is felt and carried by people who have experienced repeated or prolonged emotional deprivation in some form.

If you're reading this, you may imagine that deprivation should be obvious and dramatic in order to really be impacted by it. However, for each person affected by emotional deprivation, the threshold is different.

There are endless examples of how we can all carry pain, or even trauma, from emotional deprivation. One example is the deprivation of touch, hugs, or general affection from one or both parents throughout childhood. Another example is not feeling that one or both parents understands you, or truly cares to know who you are. Or partners or friends who don't seem to care as much about your relationship or put as much effort into them as you do. There are many forms of emotional and physical deprivation that exist.

In the starvation of needs section, I talk about how when a need is starved out that a craving develops that doesn't tend to go away.

Instead, the craving continues to persist and grow until it can't be ignored anymore, leading to breaking relationships and running to the greener grass in order to fulfill the starved need. These needs tend to be more situational. For example:

"I want someone who has more (or better) sex."

"I need someone who is more affectionate."

"I need more conversations and someone who hears me when I talk."

"I need someone who will prioritize time at home over longer work hours."

"I want someone who understands I need space to be myself."

And so on. These are clearly identified deprivations that create a strong sense of yearning and, eventually, a void that can't be tolerated any longer when they are neglected.

When someone already carries a deeper feeling of emotional deprivation or neglect historically under the surface, the deprivation can become the disease, beyond the current situation. When deeper deprivations are at play—often from upbringing at home, with peers, or otherwise—the symptoms are usually painful already. It can feel like you're yearning for something, craving it, feeling starved, like you need something so badly but aren't allowed to have it. Or, you may even feel resigned to living without certain deprivations over time.

With deeper emotional deprivation, because it goes beyond the current situation it can become difficult to feel fulfilled or satisfied for more than a short period of time without the feeling of deprivation returning. As another example, in a situational need, you may be upset that your partner doesn't want to have more sex. However, historically, if your needs are minimized by the people who are supposed to be caring for you, you may find yourself distressed by the deeper wounds that are being touched here, in addition to the lack of sex. The lonely feeling that it perhaps rarely gets to be *your* turn for what *you* need. This goes beyond the situational starved need to a chronic deprivation.

Not every need is reflective of a deeper deprivation. This is a significant difference to understand. Everyone has needs in a relationship, or where to live, or in their careers, but just because you have needs and desires does not always mean they are reflective of a deeper deprivation. Sometimes it is the case that a current situational need is amplified because of deeper deprivations, but it isn't always this way. This is how to understand the difference between a starved situational need versus hitting an old and painful point of deprivation.

When you rub up against an open wound that's been open for a long period of time, it can be hard to tell sometimes if it is so painful because the present situation is really bad, or if it's because something in the present situation touched the old wound that is still carried. When old emotional deprivations are touched, which can often happen in relationships for a number of reasons, they can be excruciating. Because of this, people often look to immediately treat the painful symptom, rather than the deeper deprivations. This leads to unhealthy reactions: distancing a relationship, breaking up, addictions and behaviors in attempt numb the pain, etc.

In short, when there is a deeper sense of deprivation underlying a disappointment, a disappointment is no longer simply a present and upsetting disappointment in the relationship. It instead holds your current relationship responsible for the old pain. It can create feelings of resentment, anger, pain, loss, betrayal, and other possible emotions that can heavily cloud and unsettle your feeling towards your current relationship when these feelings likely belong to the original offenders and those who perpetuated these points of deprivation. (This is often a type of carried emotion that people work through in therapy, so the old doesn't get in the way of the present).

When you're in the depths of being triggered, it can be very hard to separate what belongs to *then* and what belongs to *now*. In Grass Is Greener Syndrome, confusion in knowing how to attribute the pain of deprivation can actually result in the cascade towards disillusionment.

Relational Trauma

Relational trauma can often be found alongside grief and deprivations and within the greater grass is greener pattern. Relational trauma generally occurs when you've experienced mistreatment in relationships repeatedly over periods of time. This can happen when growing up with parents, with siblings, or romantic relationships; interpersonal issues with peers or friends; bullying; and in pretty much any interpersonal scenario that has a negative impact on how your relational patterns and dynamics function.

If you've been through significant relational trauma, it can actually result in complex trauma reactions, which can include having a strong impact on how close or vulnerable you may allow yourself to be in relationships with people. It can make it very hard to trust others with your emotions, or let others become close to you in various ways. When you've had a history with relational trauma, you've likely experienced repeated pain, hurt, disappointment, feelings of betrayal, worthlessness, low self-esteem, and have possibly learned that keeping relationships at an arm's distance is the safest way to have relationships.

When there is relational trauma or complex trauma in your background, it can feel like your emotional needs aren't going to be met, because what it would take to have them met makes you too vulnerable. Therefore, you end up existing in a "damned if you do, damned if you don't" position. You have emotional needs that are being starved and need them to be fulfilled. But in order to have them fed, you have to become vulnerable to the potential of emotional hurt and pain.

And after the pain you've likely already experienced, this risk can feel like too much. This deeper (usually unconscious) dilemma is often at play when in the midst of the grass is greener cycle.

Who We Are *Supposed* to Be Versus Who We *Desire* to Be

A struggle with identity can often be greater as a result of relational and complex trauma. When it becomes hard to trust your interpersonal emotional (or physical) safety, it can create a deeper conflict with your sense of self and self-actualization. As explained earlier, in Grass Is Greener Syndrome there can be a conflict happening between the experience of oneself on the outside, versus the experience of oneself on the inside.

In general—not just with Grass Is Greener Syndrome—it can be common for people to feel conflicted about who they think they're *supposed* to be and who they *desire* to be. Who they're *supposed* to be is the creation from the outside that they have learned people approve of, and what they've learned people disapprove of. These messages can come from parents, peers, society, moments of starvation, deprivation, relational trauma, greater trauma, and so on. The conflict for many people can be about who their parents may want them to be, or who others have validated are the more acceptable ways of being while growing up.

For example, think of a trait of yours that generates a positive response or that people have usually approved of or validated over the course of your life—but may not otherwise have been your own choice of character trait. This trait is something you have adopted and learned to carry because people responded to it favorably.

Or, think of a trait that you adopted because it protected you. Perhaps from an aggressive parent, or from bullies at school, or otherwise. No matter how or why you adopted these traits, for one reason or another you have likely learned at some point that these traits helped or protected you in some way. They sent a message that it is better to become what the outside world expects of you. If you do this, life will be easier for you. We all have certain parts of us that were encouraged into place by others.

Who you *desire* to be, on the other hand, is what comes from you on the inside, as opposed to the outside. Perhaps there are parts, desires, wishes, needs, or characteristics of yours that you withhold, hide, push down, repress, or suppress—knowing or worried they'd be disapproved of, or that they could put you in harm's way, or make life harder for you in some way.

When you have been through repeated forms of disapproval, criticism, and judgment in your upbringing, you can start to suppress and repress certain parts of you. Not only personality-wise, but this can go into the path you choose in life from types of relationships, to having kids or not, career choices, and more. The more criticism and judgment or disapproval, the more a person can shift externally, and try to match it internally as well.

Think about the times you were perhaps pushed to be in a certain career by your parents when you were growing up, or the times when you were scolded for a certain behavior, or when you learned to not speak up because you were picked on or criticized, etc. There are many ways the messages coming from outside can impact and reshape who we become over time. When we can integrate these shifts, there isn't always a greater fallout from it.

However, when there are enough of these messages to change our course, whether through repeated judgments, criticisms, consequences, or even enough positive reinforcements of outside traits, it can set up a great divide and a strong tension between who we feel we're supposed to be and who we actually desire to be.

This tension between buying into a set of expectations from others versus a more dedicated sense of self-actualization can result in a projection. We may constantly seek the qualities we know we're expected to have or the life we know we're expected to live—maybe this is as simple as getting married or having children because you know that's "what people do." Or it could be many other possibilities including, for one example, being "nice" all the time.

However, when this divide is too great, and the shifts cannot be fully integrated, it can set up a sense of inadequacy and even uncertainty about who you are in the face of who you're expected to be. It becomes a sense of confusion, and even a loss of identity to some extent.

Grass Is Greener Syndrome can be greatly exacerbated and supported by these projections. People who struggle in this area often try to live as they're *supposed* to live until they can no longer do it because the internal struggle is too great—consider it a deprivation of the self. When this happens, people switch sides by going to the "next" in order to nurture parts of the self, but can often become conflicted that they are doing something bad or risky by being too much of themselves, and they act out the conflict by repeating the cycle again.

Conflicted senses of identity can be a big part of the foundation of the grass is greener cycle. We can only be who we have taken on from others for so long before the internal starts to feel like it's starving and needs to be fed in a different way. And the longer we stay repressed or dissociated from these parts of ourselves—especially when the outside is living potentially in an opposing manner—the stronger this mechanism grows, and the more the cycle repeats.

Simply put, if you're living life according to what other people have created for you, there's usually only so long a person can tolerate this tension before who you are on the inside needs to breathe and have its own space to live. But then, the fear of disapproval can actually cause people to revert back the other direction, which only perpetuates the cycle. This tends to happen more when people haven't resolved the tensions between what they feel is expected from them versus who they are and want to be.

STORY #4: OLIVIA

Olivia was forty-one years old when she started working on her grass is greener struggles. She was in a stable marriage with three children. However, she had always found herself flip-flopping with her career. Olivia was highly driven and was successful when she would pursue a path, however she found it difficult to stay engaged with a path much longer than a handful of years. She would feel excited and optimistic for the first year or so in each job. She knew how to be successful, make money, and find satisfaction in her success. At least at first. Then, like clockwork, after a year or so things would slowly start changing and the doubts would take over.

This pattern would show up as slowly feeling less motivated by what she was doing, and even a bit bored. It would become harder week by week—and eventually day by day—to bring herself to feel motivated for work. She'd start to become annoyed either by the people she was working with or by the work she was doing and the expectations placed on her at work.

As this persisted and she fell more into the grass is greener cycle, she would start to feel that she needed a new career path again. It felt like once she had the career choice right that she'd feel stimulated and look forward to going to work every day.

As good as she was at her ability to create success, Olivia often felt inadequate, or like an imposter at work—especially the more responsibility she took on, the more important her role, or the more money she earned. Olivia always felt like she was waiting for people to discover that she really wasn't competent and that she was just fooling them. This mindset added a lot of pressure and stress to her daily work that would often emotionally deplete her, making it harder to feel motivated.

The way the cycle would play out was that every time she would become more successful in her work, she would start to undermine her success by seeing the job as questionable if they relied on her. The way Olivia saw it, there must be something wrong with the career or the job if they saw her as good. This became the projection—reflecting the inadequacy she experienced of herself. She felt so inadequate and certain she wasn't worthy of success that she would instead see the career as inadequate if she was able to succeed in it.

Once success would start to happen in each different path, she would start to see everything wrong with what she was doing. It began as subtle disappointments, and then would eventually cascade through the grass is greener cycle to the point that she'd leave to start another job or fully different career each time. This cascade could sometimes take a few years, but it always ended the same—with starting over.

By the time she started to address her grass is greener struggles she had already been in three careers and was now thinking about moving to a fourth. This time, however, she felt something was off about the fact that she was constantly changing careers. She didn't know the specifics of this cycle yet; she only knew that there was a pattern she was sensing. Olivia knew she wanted to settle into one career, and preferably one job, and she didn't want this repeated starting over, which was hard on her and her family.

Growing up, Olivia was in a family where her brothers were rewarded for their ability to work. Olivia, on the other hand, was usually praised for her looks and her artistic abilities, but did not receive the same level of attention for her ability to lead, think, create (beyond art), and other qualities. While she was able to succeed in all of these areas, she couldn't trust herself to accomplish the work of someone who would be paid well or succeed in a career. That wasn't the identity placed onto her growing up the way it was with her brothers.

No matter how smart she was or level of ability she possessed, the messages she received growing up made her underestimate and under-value these parts of her. Therefore, when her external value (being well paid) exceeded her lower internalized value, she would feel uncom-fortable and like an imposter. This is generally where things started to turn—any sense that she was valued or having success beyond what made sense to her.

Olivia realized in her work that her identity became more about working for the approval she couldn't get from her parents growing up. And then, when she would get it, she'd sabotage her job and start over to work for it again and again.

As she started to let go of the need for this approval from the outside and embrace her true drive and abilities, she found herself able to accept more success and feel less pressured by it. She was able to be more of who she wanted with her work and not feel like she didn't deserve success.

Olivia's story is an example of how she was at odds with who she was told from the outside she was *supposed* to be. She was driven to succeed, but she was always treated as the "pretty and artistic" one while her brothers were the seen as the ones who could succeed in a career (when, really, they apparently all had the ability to succeed, and Olivia was even more successful than her brothers in various ways.

She was also able to successfully utilize her creativity and artistic abilities in her career.).

As she was able to reconcile the differences between who she desired to be, rather than who she thought she was being pushed to be, she was able to feel less like an imposter and more connected to herself and her career choice. This has made embracing success more meaningful, rather than running from it. Though confidence issues can still arise for Olivia and she can go through heavy stress at times, she hasn't experienced a need to find another career for several years now.

CHAPTER 5

Grief

It is complicated to effectively discuss the process of grief in Grass Is Greener Syndrome. While each topic is contained in its own section or chapter in this book, every element of Grass Is Greener Syndrome in reality is woven throughout the experience of the cycle, interlocked and interconnected with each other. It isn't a step-by-step, linear process. The only linear part of Grass Is Greener Syndrome is the order of the grass is greener cycle. But everything else is tied together and plays out very differently from one person to another.

I bring this up here because grief is inextricably linked with Grass Is Greener Syndrome. A good analogy for grief's role in Grass Is Greener Syndrome is to imagine a table (for the sake of simplicity we'll say a basic table, though to be more accurate for the grass is greener process it would have more than four legs). The various legs are all the points we are discussing in each chapter.

Grief, however, would be similar to the lacquer that touches every part of the table and makes the whole table stand out more. The legs are still connected to the same unit, the table top is connected as well, but the lacquer accentuates and deepens the whole unit. The table isn't made of lacquer, so it would be a folly to overfocus on grief in working through this issue, but it would also be a folly to underfocus on it.

When it comes to the grass is greener process and patterns, there is always a deeper yearning, the feeling that something is deeply missing that would make you feel whole. A void, if you will. A void that can at times feel so deep that it can't be filled. And, even when it is filled, it's only temporary. These feelings are often attached to a longing of what once was and now can't have again.

The Heavy Grip of Nostalgia and Chasing the Past
The grip of nostalgia is important enough to have its own chapter. However, the experience of nostalgia is deeply tied to grief. When in the grip of nostalgia, every image in your mind can seem to have a glossy shine or lacquer over it, like the table. These are the experiences from the past that you may deeply yearn to reconnect with, to revisit, or to rewind time and resume that place in your life over again. Maybe to appreciate it differently, or maybe just to be back in the comfort of that time or with the people who were there, or otherwise. The void of what is lost and in the past, what is missing and no longer attainable to live as it once was, is often relived through the experience of nostalgia.

You may ask, why is this a problem? Everyone becomes nostalgic from time to time, don't they? While this is true, people who struggle with Grass Is Greener Syndrome often have a very hard time managing the cross between an element of fantasy and reality when it comes to certain experiences.

We all experience different types of losses throughout life. These can be any losses that are meaningful for you. This doesn't only mean deaths, though these are included. Perhaps the loss of parents, grandparents, or siblings. Or other meaningful people in your upbringing or adult life. The loss of your childhood, or losses that happen in divorce or the separation of families, or leaving home for school and going into the "real world." Losing the attention or affection of a parent you may have once had. Losing friends, or old meaningful geographical places such as homes you lived in, a neighborhood, or school you used to go to. Losing a period of time in your life that you wish you could return to. Images of family holidays that used to be filled with joy and people who may no longer be around. And more. Any and all losses that hold meaning become available in experiences of nostalgia.

With each loss comes an experience of grief. While some people have the support, help, or encouragement to process grief as it happens throughout life, many don't. And many carry around various forms of grief throughout life from childhood or other periods of life to an extent of feeling emotionally crushed by grief—which can lead to depression over time. The more powerful the repressed grief, often the more powerful the experiences of nostalgia.

Deep and repeated nostalgic memories tend to give people a present-day glimpse into what losses remain unprocessed. The feeling with nostalgia is generally a deep sense of craving and longing for the ideal. It feels like a heavy pull to claim (or reclaim) moments that are no longer available in the present. However, the deep pain of letting go of these points of grief can be so emotionally overwhelming that rather than going towards processing the grief, people in grass is greener patterns often try to reclaim the lost projected feeling of an experience. Generally, this craved feeling is one of euphoria and pure fulfillment, where you've found and rejoined with what you've lost. At least in fantasy, nothing can be better than this feeling.

However, this creates an idea that if you're not experiencing the euphoria that comes with reliving these memories, then where you are now in the present isn't a good enough reality. The way you imagine it would feel to be back in the time of the memory becomes the goal. When that euphoric feeling isn't realized, or is only able to be realized short-term—at the greenest grass—it can feel like you're going to be in grief and deprivation forever if you don't change your situation to find that feeling.

The pain of loss can feel so deep and so daunting internally (and unconsciously) that rather than go the direction of grieving the losses and working through the deep pain, it creates a sort of treasure hunt. A chase for the fantasy of the past. Living out and repeating the wish again and again (momentarily successfully, and then only to lose it again) that someone, or some different situation, is going to create a lasting feeling that will replace the pain of the losses, deprivation, or disappointment.

In short, rather than grieve their losses, people with Grass Is Greener Syndrome tend to keep trying to fill a previous void with a new present relationship, career, place to settle, or new life. The deeper pain of the grief is unconsciously too scary and daunting. The only way people know how to avoid grieving is to keep searching for something that will fill the void. This helps set up the repeating grass is greener cycle. And while this may avoid grief, eventually the grass is greener cycle becomes so painful because of what it does to your present life that there's no choice but to face it.

I mentioned how every memory in the grip of nostalgia seems to have a glossy shine on it. This is actually quite significant. In the present, when lost within the nostalgic memories, the level of emotion we attribute to these memories is generally heavier and deeper than they were at the time the memory was created. The nostalgic feeling can actually be quite different than the actual feelings in the past were. This is because of the grief adding its own deep yearning to the memory.

This is important because the level of emotional fulfillment we tend to search for in the grip of nostalgia is usually on a level that doesn't tend to be found in reality as much as in fantasy. The honeymoon/idealization phase of a new relationship can temporarily mimic this euphoria because it seems to fill the void, however, maintaining this feeling is a high if not unrealistic bar to set.

When You Choose, You Lose

One of the pieces of Grass Is Greener Syndrome that can feel so defeating is that there is always a rejected choice. A sacrifice, if you will. When making the decision to go towards one direction, there is always an option that you're going away from. The result of this is a loss and, therefore, some amount of grief and pain, no matter which way you choose.

For example, if you decide to end your relationship so you can find something better, you're leaving something (and someone) behind in order to take the new path. Or, if you decide it's time to move to a new city, you're leaving another behind. In these transitions, there is going to be loss and grief, and adjustments need to be made to the new. No matter how good the new may feel, in the all-or-nothing grass is greener process, there is bound to be something you're losing.

The experience of pain and grief can be a bit confusing and hard to know how to process it, or what to make of it. Often, when people experience longing, yearning, or the feeling of missing something, it can be perceived as a sign that they've gone the wrong direction. Why would you be missing the other person or place or the option you went away from if you didn't make the wrong choice? Essentially, you feel if you had made the correct decision and chosen the right path, then you wouldn't have all of these complicated yearning feelings. You'd just be happy where you are.

However, this is a flawed thought process. What is faulty is the perception that the right choice means you will only feel good. In any circumstance where there is loss of something—not just a person or place, but even just parts of the person or place that were fulfilling—there is going to be a sense of grief of what you are losing or to some degree being deprived of. Even if you are going towards something fulfilling and that makes you happy, you will still grieve the loss of the choice left behind, in one way or another.

Perhaps the relationship left behind brought something with it that isn't similar in the new relationship. Maybe the sex isn't as good, or the talking is a bit less stimulating, or the fun is different. Either way, there are losses to grieve, and just because there is pain and grief doesn't necessarily mean it's a sign that you're supposed to go back or find something better. Feeling pain, sadness, or yearning doesn't mean you made the wrong decision, as much as it can mean you're grieving what you lost.

Filling a Deep Void

You may have noticed that I keep mentioning this desire to fill deep voids, certain needs that are missing, or other emotional voids that may be creating urges to run away or seek the greener grass.

While as you're probably seeing by now there are many complex players in Grass Is Greener Syndrome, the urges to start over are often reflecting a deep void. Even though starting over fills an emotional void of some kind, with Grass Is Greener Syndrome, it generally ends up being temporary fulfillment. This tells us is that there is something about the void: It can be filled temporarily, but it keeps returning. There is a deeper, insatiable need or needs that seem to be so great that they never feel fulfilled no matter how much you actively try.

This is one of the reasons grief is such an important concept in Grass Is Greener Syndrome. The losses over time—loss of loved ones, loss of time, loss of childhood, loss of those deeply nostalgic images that can no longer be lived in the present, etc., all create emotional voids over time. Some are so deep that have never been mourned or grieved that the unconscious attempt to fill them becomes an endless pursuit of unknowingly blocking the mourning that has never happened.

When people carry grief that feels too deeply painful to connect with, instead of letting it go, we cope by trying to fill the void with thoughts and actions to keep us from having to face the emotional pain. In the process, we temporarily fill the voids, find intermittent ways to feel better, and then eventually the grief comes back, looking for acknowledgment and release that hasn't happened.

However, instead of embracing this—usually without knowing it consciously—we try to cover up the pain again. This is common with issues such as addiction, and Grass Is Greener Syndrome has this similar quality. Cover the pain and the deep void by finding a new high to numb it. It's worth noting that Grass Is Greener Syndrome has differences from addiction, so I wouldn't recommend treating it like an addiction. But the element of blocking the pain of loss in ways that work against you when you don't know what to do with the overwhelming emotions is a shared quality.

STORY #5: JASON

Jason was thirty-six when he started to address his grass is greener issues. Despite his struggles, Jason was actually fine in relationships. He had been in a relationship with his partner for twelve years. He was also satisfied with his job and career choice where he ran his own successful business. His work was tough and overwhelming at times, but he knew he was in a role that suited him well.

Jason's grass is greener struggle, however, was that he could never feel settled with where he lived geographically. He was always craving somewhere else, and it never seemed to be where he was in the present, except for short periods of time.

For a bit of background, Jason grew up in California. He moved to Chicago for college. And then after college took a job in New York City. The job sent him to London for a year when he was twenty-three. But then he moved back to New York, which is where he met his long-term partner. They aren't married and are happy with where their relationship is.

However, Jason yearned for the life he grew up with. He would often find himself daydreaming with deeply nostalgic feelings about his home in California, growing up, and envisioning that life if he and his partner decided to have kids one day (which they were uncertain about). He would visit his family in California a couple times per year, and it would never feel long enough.

Jason's nostalgic feelings would haunt him to the point of depression. He would feel weighed down by memories of family, being a kid in his backyard, going to the beach, holidays with his family, and more. After he and his partner had been together for six years, they decided to move from New York to California. At this point, Jason was thirty.

Once he was back in California, he felt whole again. Like some part of him he'd lost was able to be brought back to life. Nothing could feel better than having this feeling of deep yearning finally gratified. This lasted for a solid six months. And then, it changed.

When in New York, all of the nostalgic memories never included the things about his upbringing that were very difficult. His family was always hard for him to be around. His parents divorced when he was seven, and the stepparents on both sides were not nice to him growing up. There was often conflict within the family between him and his brother and sister, and the two sets of parents. Jason and his siblings mostly grew up with their mom and stepdad, but Jason and his siblings were often caught in the middle of the friction between the two parents.

When Jason was away at college and then creating a life in New York City, he was able to avoid the stress and frustrations of family issues. Conveniently, his nostalgic thoughts did not include the unpleasant parts of growing up (as nostalgia generally doesn't include the negatives). Now, as the disappointments of living relatively close to his family again started to weigh on him, he began to find himself craving the life he'd built for himself in New York City.

After moving out of his Northern California home to go to college, he started to figure out his own identity, was able to embrace his sexuality more openly, and find a life that fit who he was, more so than what his parents may have wanted. The life he created away from his childhood home became his new home. Now that he was back in Northern California, he found his urges increasing to return to New York to resume his life.

Jason's partner traveled for work a lot, so while it wasn't fully up to Jason, his partner wasn't opposed to another move, but Jason also knew his partner wouldn't continue to be okay with repeated moves. So, two years after moving back to Northern California, Jason and his partner moved back to New York. At this point, Jason was thirty-two.

For the next few years, things were relatively good. He knew that a life in Northern California didn't make sense, even though he still struggled with deeply nostalgic thoughts about his childhood. He would also struggle with depression on and off. As a whole, Jason carried a deep sense of grief that was never processed from various losses in his life.

However, what led Jason to finally address his grass is greener issues was that a few years after being back in New York again, he found himself with the strong urge to move to Chicago and London. Both were places where he had created many memories that he longed to relive—Chicago being the first place in his life where he was on his own, and London being a unique experience for a year after college. He knew that his partner wouldn't be okay with another big move, and Jason realized that a larger pattern was happening that he needed to understand and figure out. They both wanted to be settled down in one place and have a community they could grow with over time. And the repeated starting over was taxing for both of them.

In Jason's grass is greener process, he held on to losses very closely and deeply. These weren't just losses by death, or even people. Some were. For Jason, the losses of places he was greatly attached to, periods of life, and points in time that he could never fully have back plagued him.

As Jason worked through the deep grief and voids that he carried within himself (as well as other elements that were supporting his grass is greener cycle), he found that there was a middle ground where he could visit these places, and his family, but that just because he craved something didn't mean where he was now was the wrong choice. As he worked through his grass is greener patterns Jason found that he didn't crave the moves so much anymore. He would at times become sad or daydream, but he could do so without feeling an overwhelming urge to start over. This also helped make his visits with family more enjoyable, and also allowed him to feel more at home and settled in his present life.

CHAPTER 6

Fear of Intimacy and Commitment

Without understanding Grass Is Greener Syndrome on a deeper level, many assume at first that grass is greener struggles are synonymous with "commitment issues" since the surface level appearance looks like a struggle to commit. However, as you're probably gathering by now, there is a lot more to it than that. Many people can have issues with commitment in life without necessarily having Grass Is Greener Syndrome. But, when someone struggles with Grass Is Greener Syndrome, fear of commitment is one *symptom* that is almost always a part of it. The difference is, someone with Grass Is Greener Syndrome struggles with many of the other elements you're reading in this book in addition to the fear of commitment.

Fear of intimacy can also often work together with fear of commitment, whether inside or outside of the grass is greener cycle. Both have a significant presence within Grass Is Greener Syndrome and make the overall struggle that much more difficult. However, in grass is greener patterns, the reasons for fear of commitment and intimacy can actually look and feel different than someone who struggles with commitment and intimacy in a more isolated way outside of Grass Is Greener Syndrome.

Fear of Intimacy

Most people crave intimacy, especially when they aren't able to experience it often enough. But intimacy is complex. When people have had relational trauma in one form or another, it can become difficult to become emotionally or physically vulnerable with another person without it inducing a tremendous level of fear and shame—which can happen consciously or unconsciously. If you've experienced relational trauma, you know it can be hard to trust letting your guard down with another person. As a response, once becoming "too close," someone with a fear of intimacy might automatically pull back and retreat, effectively either creating distance in the relationship or even finding reasons to run away. People can sometimes be aware of their struggle with intimacy, but many are actually not consciously aware of their battle in this area, and they end up repeatedly retreating and acting out on their fear without realizing what's happening.

Fear of intimacy and pulling back from closeness in relationships can happen for a number of reasons. The most common are histories of rejection, judgment, abandonment, and pain caused by a previous relationship (or more than one), which can include relationships with parents, peers, or romantic partners. Fear of intimacy can also often be a result of childhood neglect, abuse, or other trauma (such as being bullied at home or elsewhere).

Fear of intimacy isn't only a fear of being hurt if you become close, it can also simultaneously be a fear of the shame of vulnerability of letting your guard down. Essentially, there is often shame in having these emotional needs for closeness in the first place. If you allow yourself to become vulnerable and let your emotional guard down with somebody, this can feel very scary, especially if you've been hurt in the past for doing so. Being in a vulnerable space—especially with an imperfect and flawed person—can be really hard. But at the same time, people still crave closeness and intimacy. So there can be a push-pull with closeness and distance. In Grass Is Greener Syndrome, this push-pull often extends to the point of starting over.

When we experience pain in our close relationships or general peer relationships, it can become a natural reaction to stay at arm's distance. Becoming close, opening ourselves up to being emotionally out of control in a relationship, and being vulnerable to another person becomes experienced as a threat rather than as a something positive. If you feel deep down that becoming close or emotionally intimate is going to end up in shame and humiliation, the instinct to retreat can overpower the desire to experience closeness. This ends up keeping relationships from growing closer.

If people have had relational traumas, when they then experience a relationship coming to a point where it's going to grow closer and become more intimate (for example, moving in together), the reaction is often to pull back and get away before they can get to that next step which requires them to become more vulnerable. The fear of pain, the worry of physical or even emotional abandonment, even the idea of eventual death—the loss that in one way or another feels sure to come—makes being known and open to another so emotionally risky that someone who fears intimacy prevents the relationship from getting to the next level.

As a result, this actually feeds the grass is greener cycle. Instead of allowing oneself to become closer in a relationship and start to commit on a deeper level, whenever the relationship hits a point where it needs to deepen and grow (or else become stagnant), someone who is fearful of intimacy may start to sabotage the relationship or the closeness in order to avoid this vulnerability. This generally happens on an unconscious level. It isn't as if they decide that it's time to sabotage things now. The reactions just start to happen instinctively. They might start finding the negatives in the relationship, looking for the problems, or envisioning the fears playing out in a way that justifies their distancing. The defenses come up, the desire to leave and start over shows up, and it fuels the cycle.

Some relationships stay in this arm's distance dynamic for long periods of time. However, many end up backing completely away and continuing the cycle of looking for the next person who's going to hopefully be the better option, instead of working through the present issues and vulnerabilities. Seeking help can make it more possible to manage these obstacles when the desire to pull back shows up, without having to fully turn back and start over.

Fear of Commitment

Commitment fears are also complex. You may strongly urge for a close and committed relationship, but find yourself balking when the idea of commitment truly presents itself. It is very difficult to commit when struggling with intimacy issues. Abandonment, trauma, neglect, and abuse are all part of fear of commitment as well. They all have their role in why it can be scary to commit.

It's not always so obvious when commitment issues stand alone or are part of Grass Is Greener Syndrome. The lines here aren't perfectly clear. What may at first seem like a commitment-only issue can later show the greater grass is greener pattern at play. However, I have worked with many people who struggle with commitment issues who don't play out the greater grass is greener patterns. Some struggle with commitment because they witnessed a bad relationship between their parents, or witnessed their parents' divorce, for example. Or, they've decided that committing to one person (or place, career, etc.) limits the life they see for themselves. It doesn't necessary fall into the cycle as much as commitment issues can be a reaction to the complexities of commitment in and of itself. This can be its own thing.

There are many possibilities when someone struggles with commitment issues. For example, it can often be a fear of what committing to one path will mean for the paths they're not choosing. What if you choose someone who ends up being the wrong person? What if the need for love and care isn't going to be enough from this one person and you are going to need others to make up for what this person can't give to you? What if you can't give the other person what they might need? What if you can't stay committed like maybe your own parents couldn't?

In these situations, it's not always about finding the better relationship, running from pain or grief, or reacting to disappointment, for example, as much as it's about the idea of committing in general, and how this in and of itself might hurt them in one way or another. It's very risky to commit when it feels like you're going to need more than one relationship can offer, or that the relationship will end up hurting you or the other. Fear of intimacy and commitment are often tied together in this way—the idea that commitment is a step in achieving greater intimacy and depth in one place, and taking this step brings the fear of some form of hurt or failure.

The main difference I see between someone who has "commitment issues" versus someone who struggles with Grass Is Greener Syndrome, aside from the repetitive grass is greener pattern, is that with commitment issues the person will often pull back from the relationship anytime they see the potential for the relationship to grow closer or to take a next big step in the relationship. This tends to be the trigger for people who struggle with commitment—to start pulling back or pushing people away from the relationship when they sense greater intimacy or commitment coming up.

With Grass Is Greener Syndrome, people generally start to pull back once they experience the disappointment and disillusionment, or the expectations are too high, or the yearning for the nostalgia and excitement takes over, etc., because they feel there is something better and more perfect or ideal out there. Disappointment, disillusionment, and devaluing the relationship often sets up the fear of commitment in the grass is greener struggle (though keep in mind that it's not always so simple or binary).

STORY #6: NAOMI

Naomi was thirty-seven years old when she started looking for help with her commitment issues and generalized anxiety. She was anxious in a number of parts of her life; however, relationships and the idea of commitment were particularly difficult for Naomi. She craved a deep, intimate relationship with a partner whom she would have a lot in common with, would have strong sexual chemistry, would be able to have deeper conversations about life together, and would look forward to spending time together. Essentially, she wanted the physical and emotional intimacy of a relationship.

However, Naomi found that she couldn't allow herself to be fully vulnerable in a relationship. She would meet someone, and at first there would be exciting and carefree sexual chemistry. They would go out and have fun together, engage in long conversations about life, and seemed to have several shared interests. Many of the ingredients Naomi looked for would be there at the start of each relationship.

At a certain point—usually within the first year and a half or so—Naomi would start to experience a shift in the relationship. She was able to handle disappointments here and there. She knew that a relationship involved imperfect people with their own flaws trying to make life work together. So, the occasional disappointments didn't send her into a grass is greener cascade.

What made relationships tough for Naomi, though, was that after a certain period of time in the relationship she would become aware that a larger commitment was looming. She knew there would eventually be talk of where things were going next—if they were going to move in together, or get married and have kids. Interestingly, these were all things that she wanted to have, but she feared these conversations and actually taking these next steps in the relationship. This was exacerbated by the fact that she'd previously moved in with two partners in relationships that ultimately failed in the past. The first time was when she was twenty-five, which lasted for two years living together before they broke up. The second partner she moved in with was when she was thirty where they broke up a year later.

In each relationship, after they moved in together things changed. The deep conversations wouldn't happen much anymore, the sex wasn't as good or as frequent, and she would start to feel burdened and constrained by the relationship. She started to notice more of the negative qualities of the person she was with, and she would even feel repelled from closeness or intimacy with each partner and found herself maintaining distance.

They'd watch TV shows together, but from opposite ends of the couch. The physical and emotional intimacy seemed to disappear as well. It was usually her partner that would initiate closeness and, even though she also wanted it, she would usually shut it down. After the first six months living together in considerable emotional distance, in both instances she started envisioning the other people she could potentially meet and be with rather than seeking that closeness with her partner. Naomi was aware enough to know that she had felt blocked to her partner, but she couldn't figure out how to emotionally let her guard down in a way that wouldn't feel intimidating, scary, or shameful.

Vulnerability in a closely committed relationship was overwhelming for Naomi. It felt like she was opening herself up to humiliation and shame, similar to how she felt growing up whenever she was passionately excited about something and then her brothers would laugh at her and make fun of her for being so excited. This always made her feel ashamed for her excitement and she came to experience her passion as a problem, or something to hide. Over the years she became more emotionally guarded in order to avoid the repetitions of shame and hurt. (There was more to her struggles with intimacy and commitment than the years of shaming by her brothers, but these experiences during such formative years were strong contributors).

Because of these deeper issues with commitment and intimacy, Naomi would leave her relationships before they could reach marriage. Living together was already a level of closeness that caused her to emotionally retreat from her relationships, so the idea of marriage felt almost intolerable. Yet, at the same time, there was still a pull in the other direction of a life she wanted to have that involved a committed relationship and possibly a family. Naomi knew that in order to get there she had to overcome these issues with intimacy and commitment.

Now, in her current relationship that brought her to address her struggles, Naomi is living with her partner. However, she's constantly thinking about breaking away and starting over. Naomi fears she will end up trapped in a loveless, distant relationship that lacks the closeness and passion that she craves. She doesn't necessarily believe it'll be easier with anyone else, which is part of the reason she hasn't left. But she's also afraid of continuing to feel distanced and disconnected in her relationship.

As she's worked on the repeated experiences of shame she received growing up that have been blocking intimacy—while also working through the impact of witnessing the distant marriage her parents had, along with other elements of anxiety contributing to her commitment and intimacy fears—Naomi has been able to go to greater depths in her current relationship. She has also been learning how to hold, tolerate, and be open to intimacy in the present without it feeling so threatening.

Naomi is now more open and freer within herself to be seen, vulnerable, and known for her passions, and to advocate for her needs from her partner. While her partner is also a person with flaws, the communication between their shared flaws actually adds to their intimacy together. Naomi has been able to stay with two feet in the door more now than she has been able to in the past.

As mentioned earlier, commitment and intimacy struggles can be their own intertwined issues separate from Grass Is Greener Syndrome or they can be symptoms of it. Sometimes, however, it is quite blurry. There can be multiple elements of Grass Is Greener Syndrome but, for example, the cycle may be a bit different (though still ending with starting over). Naomi's example shows that you don't always have to know specifically if you're dealing fully with Grass Is Greener Syndrome to know you need help becoming unstuck in a self-defeating pattern. If you see yourself starting over and struggling to feel satisfied in relationships, it's generally worth looking into.

CHAPTER 7

Decision-Making Paralysis

Should you stay or should you go? This is the typical question and decision you're faced with in some form in every grass is greener struggle. Should you start over again and look for something better, or should you stay where you are and potentially feel you're settling for less than you need? When in the active grass is greener cycle, the decision generally tends to be to start over. This means looking for the new relationship, starting on a new career path, or finding a new place to settle, or otherwise.

However, there is an underside to Grass Is Greener Syndrome that people don't often give as much credit or attention to because it is far less active, and much more passive. This is what I refer to as "grass is greener paralysis."

I Can't Decide

Another significant if not torturous symptom of Grass Is Greener Syndrome is how difficult it can be to make decisions. It can be so hard to make decisions—especially bigger life decisions—that it can almost feel like your ability to make good decisions for yourself is broken. Making decisions in the midst of grass is greener paralysis can feel nearly impossible, because it feels like no matter what you choose, you're going to be neglecting another part of yourself and what you need. With every gain there is generally a loss. A path not chosen. These losses can feel impossible to tolerate as a cost of the gains.

Grass is greener paralysis is the other extreme of Grass Is Greener Syndrome. The greater process involves chronically severing relationships of one kind or another and starting over. But, grass is greener paralysis is essentially when the ability to make bigger decisions shuts down.

At a certain point in the grass is greener process, generally after several if not many repetitions of the cycle, people may start to catch on to the fact that the same pattern keeps playing out: Relationships never feel good enough and they become disappointing; after a certain amount of time in a new career, job, or place you may yearn to either go back to where you were before or find somewhere new to start over. No matter which way you are pulled, you may eventually start to notice there is a repeating pattern pulling yourself away from the present situation.

This realization can actually cause an internal flip. Instead of repeatedly starting over, people become paralyzed from making any decision at all, and stay in perpetual uncertainty with one foot constantly out of the door.

At times, there can be a brief middle ground that happens in decision-making, which is often a sign of the flip happening. You may still make a decision, but *after* a decision is made you might feel unsettled, uncertain, and regretful. When in this middle space, it's not uncommon for people to undo their decisions. For example, you may break up with someone, but then soon after find yourself trying to go back, knowing it was a mistake to break up. Sometimes this uncertainty and regret can start right away after making a decision. Or, at first a decision can still feel good, and then later on the regret of the decision starts to show up without playing through the full grass is greener cycle.

This middle space, however, often gives way to full decision-making paralysis. After determining enough painful decisions didn't work out the way you hoped, and experiencing exhausting and overwhelming feelings of regret, shame, and inadequacy that may come with these decisions, you may eventually begin to lose trust and confidence in your ability to make the best decisions for yourself.

When you go through enough pain from decisions that haven't worked out for you, the trust and confidence in your own decision-making can become damaged, or even severed. This ultimately makes it really hard to rely on your own instincts and to trust that you really have a full sense of what's in your own best interest.

Living Between Worlds

What happens in grass is greener paralysis is that people end up hanging out in between points of decision, with one foot chronically out the door. You may derive a sense of safety from living in indecision, which feels like the only way to not make another mistake. Avoiding decisions basically becomes more tolerable than the thought of causing more pain with another failed decision. Therefore, the space where no decisions are made—life between the two worlds—is determined to be the least risky.

It's important to keep in mind, however, that even though this space of indecision and passivity is the safest space to exist, there is still the strong pull to any other points of decision that are being avoided. The between-worlds space generally isn't comfortable. It's often torture because it can feel like you need what you're not getting, but you don't know which way is up anymore. It is a sense of being paralyzed and stuck while being simultaneously pulled in different directions, and can have the effect of being a passenger in your own life. Simply said, you may have stopped physically starting over, but mentally and emotionally there's still a significant part of you that's trying to go somewhere else when in grass is greener paralysis. Why does this happen?

Even within the paralysis, there is still an emotional craving to have the new and shiny green grass, which keeps one foot out of the door. However, there is also the rational awareness that the changes and starting over haven't been working out in your favor. And, there are at least *some* positives where you are currently. This helps keeps one foot in the door.

Some may ask: Isn't this good if you are not running and repeating the cycle again? Isn't it progress to recognize that there is something "good enough" in the present and not run again to try for perfection?

This is a complicated but worthwhile question. There is a bit of both in it. This paralysis in between worlds appears to serve a function (whether consciously or unconsciously) of attempting to stop the grass is greener cycle from playing out. That can be seen as progress. It's often the only way someone can control Grass Is Greener Syndrome when they don't have more to work with yet.

However, the difficult piece is that in this type of paralysis, it is very hard to feel anything other than disappointment, starvation, deprivation, and often, depression. Because both worlds have something you truly feel you need and can't do without, and you can't have them both. Therefore, even if you're staying and not running, it likely doesn't feel fulfilling. Instead, it's often more of a sense of resignation. It feels like you just can't decide what to do on an ongoing basis— and it often feels like no matter what you decide that you'll end up regretting it once the honeymoon ends anyway. Living in between two worlds tends to be isolating and lonely, and it can often be experienced as being trapped in a prison of one's own indecision.

It's worth mentioning that just because you may struggle with decision-making in your life doesn't necessarily mean you are in the grass is greener cycle. You may need help with decision-making in general. However, keep in mind other things can lead to decision-making issues. For example, people struggle all the time with making decisions that have negative consequences at work, or in friendships, or with their partner, or in dating, or with time management, etc. There is no shortage of ways that regrets with decision-making can lead to a paralysis of making decisions.

However, the concept behind grass is greener paralysis is that you're still in the overall grass is greener struggle. You're just on the other side of the coin than when you're repeatedly running, starting over, and acting out your struggles. Now the struggle happens only on the inside without actually changing your outside circumstances. Whichever side of the coin you're on, though, the struggle is still happening.

Affairs, Guilt, and Regret

People stuck in the grass is greener paralysis part of Grass Is Greener Syndrome are often the most prone to affairs and infidelity. Not being able to commit to a decision in either direction—whether to put two feet in the door or to leave—tends to make people feel trapped and unfulfilled.

Also, people who struggle with guilt and regret can often be the most vulnerable in this area. They may go back and forth between not wanting to leave and hurt their partner in the process, or they know they may personally regret making one more mistake by leaving another situation. Yet, at the same time, they are also starved of a kind of fulfillment that it feels they can only find on the outside of the current relationship. It can often seem like a choice between guilt for hurting the other, or regret that will come later.

Therefore, people in this position between two worlds can often feel their only choice is to have an affair. This usually happens in desperation when they are starving and need the pieces of fulfillment they are missing but also can't cope with leaving. Leaving doesn't feel like a tolerable option to anyone in this position. Whether they feel a moral obligation to stay in the relationship, or because they don't trust their decision-making process, or because they know once they decide to leave that they will feel regretful of the decision and guilty for the pain they are causing (which is generally a deeper issue to explore and understand), or otherwise—people in the paralysis often realize that the grass is greener cycle is going to pull them right back even if they leave. This often can lead to cheating out of fear the deprivation will overtake them (similar to a feeling they will emotionally die of starvation, seeing no way out other than to eat now, however possible).

When you are stuck in what seems like a prison of misery and deprivation, it can feel that no matter what you do you won't be happy. Affairs can often be experienced as the last resort to save yourself from the pain of leaving, or from the pain of staying and grieving the losses that come with the decision. It is also worth noting that guilt and grief are heavily intertwined.

The affair can also be a self-fulfilling prophecy. The idea of making the decision to leave the relationship can be so scary that sometimes people will have an affair to (at least unconsciously, if not consciously) be caught, and then their partner can make the decision for them to end the relationship. This can be a way of passing off the responsibility of the decision that they can't emotionally handle—it's more tolerable to be the one left rather than face the guilt and potential regret of doing the leaving. Interestingly, though, the affair actually tends to cause the guilt and regret they feared so much. Either way, when someone is in the grass is greener paralysis, having someone else make the decision, even one that hurts, can become the relief.

STORY #7: THOMAS

Thomas reached out for help with his struggles when he was forty years old, while in the depths of grass is greener paralysis. Throughout his life, Thomas was always looking for the next dating and sexual partner. There was a thrill and a high that would come from always knowing that he was going to have a next partner— someone new whom he didn't know yet—which felt mysterious and exciting. He would commit to one woman here and there for some time, and while it was always exciting and hopeful at first, he would inevitably start thinking about when he was going to meet the next woman.

These urges would often start slowly and then cascade into what felt all-consuming. He always felt guilty for having these urges, but they occupied his mind to the extent that in a number of relationships he would leave in order to date again. Sometimes, he would have new sexual partners before leaving the relationship in order to help him out the door. For Thomas, the affair was a way of making the decision. He would cheat in order to validate the leaving, rather than cheating in order to be caught. It's important to point out though that this was done in the active starting over cycle, not from grass is greener paralysis.

However, as Thomas neared forty, he began to experience a sense of conflict. Even with this part of him that had such a strong and insatiable desire for the "next," Thomas also knew he always wanted a family, and he was aware that he couldn't continue this pattern of dating and always looking for the next woman if he was going to settle down. This part of him wanted to commit and have an intimate relationship with one woman that they could develop together over time. It was a difficult internal dissonance that often left him tense with conflict and indecision.

When Thomas was thirty-six years old, he met Rebecca. At the time he started addressing his decision paralysis, Thomas had been seeing Rebecca for about four years, during which he would have nagging cravings that would often make him doubt the relationship. At times, he would feel certain that Rebecca was the best he was going to find, and then he would switch to doubting and wondering if Rebecca was really the best he was going to find. This was a never-ending back-and-forth that emotionally exhausted Thomas.

While he was happy with the relationship and felt she was the best partner he had been with up to that point, he was struggling with the fact that their sex and intimacy life wasn't great. They didn't have sex very often, and even when they did he found it to be average compared to the excitement and thrill of a new person. Before he could get married, though, Thomas needed to be sure that Rebecca was the "perfect" partner. These two voices—the one that knew she was enough, and the one that needed better—would continue to butt against each other, almost feeling torturous at times.

In the past, when reaching this point and the cravings persisted, this is when Thomas would generally stray from the relationship, leave, and start over. Each time this happened throughout his twenties and early thirties, he wondered why his relationships were never good enough to put two feet in the door. He noticed that after he would break up, a short time later he'd often urge to return to the woman he left (though they all either wouldn't take him back or they'd already moved on by the time he would try). So the "next" he craved was sometimes actually a woman he'd already been with before.

This time, however, Thomas knew he couldn't just leave. He did care about Rebecca and part of the stress for him was the guilt he knew he'd feel if he hurt her and left her on her own. This was alongside knowing that he didn't want to leave her, but needed a way to have this urge for the next sexual partner fulfilled.

The not leaving was a positive step. He saw the pattern he was experiencing was a problem. He was trying to stay in it and commit, but there was still this internal battle that couldn't be satisfied—this other fantasy voice of what he "could" have constantly fighting the reality of what he did have. This voice would fantasize about all of the excitement, sex, and euphoria he was going to miss out on if he didn't leave Rebecca. But he still knew he'd regret it and likely want her back in a few months even if he did leave.

This battle would show up almost every day, even though there were moments that it wasn't so loud. On a rational level he knew that staying made sense, and at the same time his emotions couldn't fully align. A part of him assumed that once he found the perfect person that he would feel emotionally settled, without this ongoing ambivalence. But he was starting to doubt this idea with how long the pattern had been going on in his life.

This is the grass is greener paralysis in action. The loss of either world is too scary to go one direction or the other. Losing Rebecca would be devastating because he knew he'd likely regret it. At the same time, losing the exciting world where he could endlessly go to the next woman was also too scary.

In staying with Rebecca, Thomas wasn't only facing losing the excitement of the next sexual partner, he was also faced with grieving the loss of a part of himself that had sustained him for most of his adult life. To Thomas, the idea of losing that world meant he would end up in a marriage where he would either eventually cheat to find excitement, or otherwise face becoming a deprived, lifeless shell of himself. He wasn't sure he knew how to find excitement and joy in other forms.

The grass is greener paralysis—living in between both worlds without a clear decision—was the only way he could manage to safely exist without grief or deprivation. This existence between the two worlds wasn't a conscious decision on Thomas's part. He would continue in his relationship, all the while with one foot out the door, wondering if this was really the right relationship. By not actually deciding, he wouldn't have to grieve the intolerable loss of the path not chosen, and he also could keep the hope of the fantasy alive. It was the perfect setup for decision paralysis.

As Thomas continued working on his paralysis, he and Rebecca got engaged and then married. And while one side of him was genuinely excited and happy for this, the fantasy voice still couldn't be fully satisfied.

As he progressed, Thomas began to realize that he could never feel emotionally safe to put everything into one person. The vulnerability and risk of being hurt was too great. At one point in his mid-twenties, he had fallen in love with a woman who cheated on him and left him, leaving him devastated. As a result, since then he would always push his deeper emotional cravings to the "next" woman. The "next" was the safest place for his desire to be—where he couldn't be disappointed and hurt in the present. Of course, this also resulted in always having one foot chronically out the door.

As he addressed his fear of letting go and of loss (past, present, and perceived future loss), Thomas eventually found that he was no longer craving the "next" so much anymore. He was finding more of an internal sense of home with Rebecca, which led to more closeness and sexual satisfaction between them. The fantasy voice that sometimes wanted a new partner seemed to quiet down to the point that even when it showed up in moments, it wasn't very loud or persuasive anymore. It wasn't completely gone, but it no longer held much weight, which gave him the room he needed to find fulfillment in the present.

CHAPTER 8

I'm Struggling. How Do I Know What It Is?

A common question people ask is how to know if they are experiencing Grass Is Greener Syndrome or if they're just needing an appropriate change in some aspect of their life. This is a good question.

First, it's important to acknowledge that there is nothing wrong with making changes. It's your own life and how you choose to live your life is up to you. Some people prefer to move around and make intermittent changes, not fully settling down into one relationship, or one place, or one career, or lifestyle. For people who prefer this, having different experiences is part of their fulfillment in life and is how they generally find a sense of satisfaction. It's part of their adventure—starting over in new places, or having different jobs, and experiencing a range of relationships. This book, and the concept of Grass Is Greener Syndrome, shouldn't be taken as a form of judgment of this lifestyle.

The issue we're looking at here is when you *want* to be able to settle down, but you are finding yourself unable to feel satisfied in certain areas of life on a cyclical basis. You may want to settle down, but the relationships never seem to be right or good enough, and you are becoming disappointed after they at first seemed so good and now can't find a way through the disappointments.

The problem in this scenario is that you're actually wanting to be settled, but can't seem to find the conditions that ever feel good enough to commit longer term without looking for the way out. You end up constantly looking for the right or best option and you can't seem to find it. So, you either end up starting over again, or you stay where you are but are disappointed, frustrated, defeated, unfulfilled, and maybe even depressed. This is quite different from a choice of lifestyle that involves periodic change.

What's Motivating the Desire for Change?

Another part of determining whether your current situation is needing change or if it's a grass is greener issue is where the motivation is coming from. Obviously, if you're in an abusive relationship, or a relationship that is chronically negative and unsupportive, or causing you pain on a frequent basis, then a change would likely make reasonable sense in terms of your own safety or mental and emotional health. If you're living in a place or at a job where you clearly feel like you're trying to fit a square peg into a round hole, then a change would probably be worth considering (though if this feeling happens repeatedly then it's probably worth looking into why this keeps repeating).

If you're in a situation where very few of your overall needs are being met, this is also something to understand and consider. If your relationship seems "fine" overall, but deal-breaker needs are not being met in the relationship, or if you are certain your current relationship cannot meet your most important needs, then this may be a relationship issue that needs to be looked at further. It's reasonable that changes within the relationships or even starting over could become necessary. Again, though, if the same issues keep repeating from one situation to the next, then it's worth looking into why similar struggles keep repeating for you. Either way, it is important to have help in sorting things out if you're feeling stuck, whether or not it's specifically a grass is greener issue.

If you are living in a place or have a career that doesn't make sense to who you are, or you're not happy with the community, the environment, the politics, the work-life balance, or a number of elements that can make a place or a job undesirable, then considering a change may be reasonable. Significant life changes can be healthy, if not fully necessary, at times. It should be noted that not all necessary changes require starting over, even if some do.

However, if you start to notice a pattern to the desire or actions of starting over, and that no relationships feel good enough to settle into longer term when you're wanting to settle down, then there's more to understand about why this may be happening. It can also become a pattern to be aware of if you start noticing you're frequently seeing the negative in your relationships or situations. This is where it becomes tricky. You may find all the reasons the place you live or your career is a problem, or why your relationship isn't good. It's important here to be aware of the pattern of noticing all of the bad parts. If you find yourself looking for excuses to leave something, it sounds like help may be needed to sort out if there is a pattern or reaction happening within you, or if the current situation itself is indeed problematic and change is needed.

It is common for certain underlying issues (such as commitment or issues with intimacy) to create self-fulfilling prophecies and self-sabotage. This can often play out by only seeing the negative and finding excuses to leave or end relationships. The reasons that are found in these moments all feel very legitimate. They often come up the most when you start to feel closer in the relationship, or like a next step is about to be taken, or other intimidating situations which can produce a range of internal responses. It can be easy to start creating distance and pushing away when fears come up. This is a time to question if change is actually needed, or if the urge to change is because of deeper fears.

Also, if you notice that you're trying too hard to "have it all," this is another area to keep an eye on. Again, relationships may not work out for various reasons. But if you notice a pattern of feeling like things are good but not good enough, you could start to question if you're trying too hard to reach a type of perfectionism that's common with Grass Is Greener Syndrome.

Overall, it's better not to get too caught up in trying to fully figure out if what you're experiencing is or isn't Grass Is Greener Syndrome. I've had people come to me highly stressed and stuck in a loop trying to figure out if they have Grass Is Greener Syndrome, when it's clear they are struggling either way. The rule of thumb to follow in understanding if you should have help and look more into what you're going through is: If you feel your life and potential fulfillment is being negatively impacted, and you're struggling to find your way through it, it's likely worth having someone help you find the path forward.

Beyond the Big Three

Throughout this book, we've only really discussed Grass Is Greener Syndrome in three major areas: relationships, career/job, and where to live. The reason we're focused in these main areas is because this is where people tend to feel the impact of the grass is greener struggle the most. However, there are other ways grass is greener tendencies can show up in life.

In the previous chapter we looked at how decision-making paralysis can show up on the underside of Grass Is Greener Syndrome. One question I've often received from people is how the grass is greener process can impact people's decisions in other areas of life and how broadly it can be applied to different types of decision-making.

These are good and also complex questions. The reality is that life is full of difficult decisions all the time. These can show up in various forms, including commitments of any kind, or how you choose the meals you eat, what show to watch, what event to do for a birthday gathering, how to handle an aging parent, if you should go to that optional work event, which house to buy, and so on. The list of decisions in life never really ends.

What is relevant to look at with Grass Is Greener Syndrome are the ways that decisions often may seem good at the start, but then later end up turning into disappointment and regret, whether soon after or further down the road. If you are often making decisions and then eventually regretting them, or if you feel so afraid of the regret that you become paralyzed from making the decision at all, this becomes relevant in the grass is greener process.

The ability to make decisions and to be able to then manage the results of that decision is a skill in and of itself that people often come to therapy to learn how to navigate. But just because you may not be good at decision-making doesn't necessarily mean you struggle with Grass Is Greener Syndrome. Decisions can be difficult for everybody at times.

It's important with decisions that after they are made people learn to manage what comes after. Maybe it goes in a good direction, maybe it doesn't, or maybe it does at first and changes later, or maybe it's a mix. But with grass is greener tendencies, going back to the decision and trying to undo it becomes the repeated pattern. You don't manage the moving forward as much as you regret the decision. This causes future decision-making to become an attempt at resolving the previous issue over and over, rather than learning how to manage the decision, both practically in the world, but also emotionally within yourself.

STORY #8: ARIANA

Ariana was twenty-nine years old and stuck at a crossroads when she started her therapy. She was recently out of a relationship, however still occasionally in communication with her ex. They would see each other once every few weeks, and would talk maybe once a week or so. But they officially were not together anymore after approximately a two-year relationship.

Ariana struggled heavily not only with relationships, but with the grander idea of what her life was supposed to look like. This made it hard for her to be able to find and sustain a long-term relationship since the idea of what she wanted a relationship to look like was heavily based on the path she wanted her life to take.

Ariana essentially lived two lives. She was a successful actor and performer who would travel often, and she also had a flexible full-time job and more low-key life where she lived. On one hand, she envisioned living a more adventurous and spontaneous life, where she could travel for work and leisure when desired; and, she also craved a more traditional and stable life where she'd have kids and be close to home more, or at least more local in how she would work and live her life. She had been able to make both lives work for a while, but she was exhausted by the back-and-forth and wanted to commit to a lifestyle and path so she could develop the chosen path further.

Ariana's regular, stable job was hybrid where she had to be in the office a few days per week but could also work from home a couple days per week. However, Ariana occasionally landed acting roles that took her away from home to film or perform (which she was able to arrange with her other job to work remotely when this would come up). She loved this adventure of being able to be in different places for weeks at a time and then be back home for a period of time before doing it again.

As she was reaching thirty and she saw more success from her life as a performer, it drove her desire for a relationship with someone who didn't want kids and would be a partner in traveling the world together. But when things were slower in the performance world, she found herself more focused on a life in a smaller, more private world with her more immediate circle where she lived, and she felt the urge to have a family. Needless to say, Ariana felt like she had to completely choose (and reject) one life. While some might say why not do both, it felt to Ariana like several main elements of each life couldn't easily or reasonably coexist.

This back-and-forth struggle left her in a position of starting relationships only to eventually break up with them every time the life path pendulum swung in a different direction. There seemed to be no end to this cycle. She was successful enough to keep her acting dream alive, but she was also between two worlds enough to not quite know which direction made sense to commit to as a lifestyle. And while there was a possibility that she could keep moving from one to the other, she knew she also craved a home and stability in her life that felt disrupted every time she did go to the exciting, more adventurous life.

A pattern that caught Ariana's attention is that she would break up from relationships, and then she would remain involved with them at a distance—almost as if she was keeping them on hold until the pendulum would swing in her life again. This would go on for months after breakups until finally her exes would have enough of waiting for her to come around and would leave. Once they left, she immediately would feel like she wanted them back, and it would make her question her life choices as a whole.

To Ariana, if she wanted a person back, it must mean that she also wanted the lifestyle back that fit that relationship. Ariana was constantly in and out of this crisis since her early twenties. This idea of which life path, and bouncing back-and-forth between them, had actually paralyzed her from fully moving forward down either path, even though her acting career was blossoming.

One could almost say this is the ultimate grass is greener struggle. There was not only a constant starting over with relationships that happened based on her career movement, but also a whole shift in life path from one life to another that would come with her relationships. They were fully intertwined.

The reality was, neither life felt like it was enough for Ariana. While some people could be happy to move back and forth between these two lives, for Ariana she just wanted to choose one and commit to it. Living in between both felt destabilizing and disorienting to her, and it felt like she was only giving part of herself to each life. Even when performing was working out, she found herself wishing for a smaller life, and when she was having the smaller life, she craved the spotlight and the freedom to move about the world again.

In her recently ended relationship, being with her partner meant choosing a family life that she was uncertain about because she worried about feeling trapped in a relationship that couldn't give her enough excitement and passion to fulfill her. At the same time, fully leaving the relationship behind felt too painful. But choosing the larger, exciting life meant that she was going to give up the more typical family life she'd imagined since she was a child.

During the course of working through this, Ariana decided that she just wanted to make a decision and commit to it—so she decided to remain single for a while and pursue her dreams of performing and traveling. And she did this and enjoyed it with good intentions.

However, after a year or so, she started to crave a relationship and the smaller life again. Even though she wanted on one hand to stand by the intended commitment, she knew that the pull towards a family life was too strong to ignore, which left her in the grass is greener conflict again of having to choose a lifestyle.

Over time, as Ariana achieved more and more success in performing, she started to realize that the life of constantly moving around wasn't actually all that exciting to her. She enjoyed it, but it felt like each time she left to play a role that she was really just escaping from her other life.

She began to realize that the life of being a performer for her was really trying to fill a deep void that she was never going to fill by always running away to play someone else. Ariana lost her father due to cancer when she was an early teen. There were two significant things that stood out to her when she recalled this time of her life. The first was that her dad always told her growing up that he thought she'd be a fantastic actor. And, secondly, she recalled the extended period of time where she and her family cared for him as he got sicker over the course of a year until he ultimately died.

She realized that the idea of committing to a life with one partner was incredibly scary when she had no control over the other person. Would something happen to them? Would they leave, or worse, die? Was she going to be left caring for another ailing person? Deep down, she worried that if she got into a relationship that she would be inadequate to care for her partner and she would lose them— the responsibility she felt for not being able to adequately keep her father alive (even though it wasn't her responsibility or her fault). It was all too scary to trust.

The life she set up for herself going back and forth between lives made it so she could have relationships, but then get as far away from them as possible once she would either sense a next step coming, or when she would start to feel inadequate and too small in the relationship. She'd then look for the escape to the life where all of her fulfillment came from performing and she didn't need anything else.

She also began to understand that while she loved acting and performing, that a big part of her was trying to make her father proud by living the life he always saw for her. And while this was meaningful to her in some way, she also realized that she was living his dream and not her own, and how painful it felt to pursue her own desired life out of worry her father would have been disappointed in her.

This is sort of a reverse grass is greener cycle. When she would experience disappointment or inadequacy within herself, she would experience a disillusionment and devaluation of who she was within her own life and, as a result, would keep switching to a new life role (not just an acting role). Therefore, the issue wasn't just the partner or lifestyle not being enough, it was more the fear that she herself was never going to be adequate enough to successfully handle either life or relationship.

This kept her in the decision-making paralysis of not committing while simultaneously and repeatedly jumping back and forth. Ariana basically set up short-term relationships and short-term lifestyles, which was only led to avoidance of long-term commitment in either area. (Ariana also played out the grass is greener cycle fully in each relationship, beginning with disappointment through starting over. Even if the inadequacy was going on within herself, she would project it outwardly at her partners and her lifestyle each time.)

Ariana realized she was setting impossible expectations for herself, her life, and her relationships as a sort of self-fulfilling prophecy— an unconscious way of keeping away from anything that could cause abandonment, rejection, pain, or loss. If she kept switching between lifestyles, then there was never a loss to deal with because she'd just go the other way whenever the fear of loss (or ultimately grief) started to show up. This impossible setup essentially made it so no one person or lifestyle could ever be good enough, and she'd have no choice but to keep leaving and starting over.

Ariana now occasionally performs and travels for short periods of time, but quite selectively. With work through the issues described above, she has found that performing is a hobby that she can visit every so often (for herself, and also with meaningful connection to her father) without feeling the pressure to have to cover or avoid the grief of losing her father, and without the pressure or guilt to live out his dream in order to still feel connected to him—knowing he loved her no matter what she did in her life.

Ariana finds that she is more emotionally stable and fulfilled by feeling at home in her life and relationship rather than always running to trying to find another life. Each time she ran away to start over, even if it was at first exciting, it always resulted in inconsistency, uncertainty, and instability for her, and was never actually enough to fill the void created by the loss of her father, and the feeling of responsibility she felt in his loss.

She ended up seeing someone new, who she's now been with for four years, and they have successfully lived together for the last two years. Disappointments do come up, and rather than running to a new person or the other life, she is learning to trust in herself and in the relationship, and to manage the fears and deeper wounds that do occasionally come up within herself. She has the same full-time job as before that she also finds meaningful for her life. When the inadequacies do show up, they are no longer so overpowering.

CHAPTER 9

Overcoming Grass Is Greener Syndrome

People have often asked me over time if I can just tell them the "secret" or "trick" to overcoming Grass Is Greener Syndrome. I wish it were so simple that I could say one thing and it would magically resolve the issue for everyone. I'm aware of the urgency and anxiety that anyone would feel when stuck in this cycle, whether in the active starting over cycle or in the paralysis. Hopefully after reading up until this point, you at least have a better sense that this struggle has likely been growing for a while if you're in the midst of it now.

It is common for people who struggle with Grass Is Greener Syndrome to sometimes attempt to force a decision to either commit to their current situation, or decide to just start over and move on. The hope being, whichever they choose they will make a concerted effort to stay with that decision and block out the other as an option. It's sort of a sense of putting your head down, turning off the emotions, and just picking one side while pledging to not give the other option attention.

For example, some say, "I'm just going to stay with my partner, and that's the decision I'm making." In the process of making this decision, they aim to shut out and defeat the doubts with an emphatic choice. The hope is that if they just pick a side and commit to it that they can overcome the grass is greener process without having to really address it. It's more of a "just do it" mindset. While the intentions are well-meaning, unfortunately it seldom works out so cleanly. This is often where people first contact me for help—once they see a forced decision is not really helping to get out of the greater cycle.

In the moment, making a decision can feel quite empowering. And to be clear, I'm not suggesting that you should do the opposite either—I'm not indicating the answer is just to break up, or to do nothing. However, once people see that forcing a decision doesn't tend to work, they often fall into defeat, resignation, and potentially depression and hopelessness.

Therefore, it is important to keep in mind that overcoming Grass Is Greener Syndrome isn't generally about "which" decision to make. Making it about "which one" plays right into the issue. Grass Is Greener Syndrome is very much a cycle that needs to be worked through and undone—without playing out the same cycle in the process. Without undoing the cycle, the cycle tends to keep going. Therefore, it often takes help for people with Grass Is Greener Syndrome to overcome it. For the most part, people who have struggled with this issue only know how to respond from within the cycle, which often really only strengthens it.

Try to keep in mind that you're dealing with a larger pattern. It can be very tempting and easy to become overly focused on the circumstance you're in right now, to the point that it becomes about the commitment or the starting over. However, the grass is greener process actually happens between these two extremes. The space between those two decisions is where the grass is greener process needs the attention and the care. That's where the work is done to overcome the cycle.

When trying to shut down that process by just going to one side or the other, almost inevitably the deprivation and starvation of needs will start to set in again because of whatever you're missing. It becomes stronger and stronger until it's almost impossible to ignore. Once this deprivation, disappointment, disillusionment, and devaluation shows up again, it then tends to become hard for people to remember why they made the attempt at the emphatic commitment in the first place. The pain of the new deprivation often overrides the well-intentioned decision to put their head down and just choose a side.

Grass Is Greener Syndrome is generally experienced as black-and-white and all-or-nothing. Middle ground is very hard to find in the midst of this cycle. Either you're satisfied, fulfilled, and getting everything you want, or you're sitting in increasing amounts of deprivation until you're starved emotionally to the point of hopelessness. The answers in this mindset tend to be either "right" or "wrong." And in grass is greener patterns, the solutions aren't usually an issue of right decision or wrong decision. It's more about what is creating this binary setup in the first place.

By the time someone first starts to play out the grass is greener patterns in their lives, it is a mechanism that has been entrenched for some time—often growing and coming together throughout childhood and adolescent years. When someone has been unknowingly living in these patterns for years, it is hard to simply break the pattern without first becoming aware of the ways that your internal patterns are acting to reinforce your grass is greener cycle every day.

Another difficulty with Grass Is Greener Syndrome is that it tends to be all-consuming when you're caught in it. When in this urgency for change, and also feeling emotionally starved, it is quite difficult to have a clear decision-making process. If you're in the thick of the tug-of-war, decisions will be made based on the distress of the tug-of-war, rather than what you're fighting about in the first place. The decisions that are made in the states of anxiety, distress, and deprivation can often be reactive and impulsive.

When you allow yourself the space to slow down and start to reflect on and understand what's going on, you have the power to work through and release the emotional patterns that have been supporting Grass Is Greener Syndrome.

What You Can Do
Having read through this book, hopefully by now you've started to notice which elements of Grass Is Greener Syndrome seem to resonate with your experience. Like I said, it's okay if only some of what you read resonates. The stories of each person written about in this book are examples of elements of Grass Is Greener Syndrome, but they are incredibly simplified. It's not easily linear, or one-to-one in the way the examples may make it appear. Also, not every part of Grass Is Greener Syndrome is detailed in this book.

Grass Is Greener Syndrome can appear quite differently from one person to the next, with different combinations of traits. For example, you may resonate more strongly with the grip of nostalgia and the pull it has on you, whereas someone else may resonate more heavily with the level of expectations that are holding them back (even if both are present for each). Most people identify with a bunch of the traits of this struggle, but for each person the degree to which each impacts them varies. Some elements may be undeniably up front, while others may be happening more in the background (and even in the background can unconsciously still have a heavy impact). Other elements may not be as significant a part of the struggle for you. For now, just start to notice what seems to feel familiar to your experience and catches your attention. From there, you can start the process of moving forward.

How I Work with You

Because Grass Is Greener Syndrome has not previously been researched or understood on a more in-depth level, grass is greener issues have often gone unrecognized and been treated more as a one-dimensional issue. Based on the accounts I've received from people who came to me after previous therapies, therapists often may treat it as a "relationship issue" or a "commitment issue" or an issue with learning how to make a decision (rather than understanding what makes a decision so emotionally complex). Grass Is Greener Syndrome generally hasn't been understood as a greater overall system that sustains itself with each repetition of the cycle.

The way that I work with this issue takes into account everything you've seen in this book, as well as things that weren't included here. It isn't a step-by-step or systematic approach. The way we work always depends on where you are in your process and what you bring in with you. What shapes this overall issue is different for each person, as everyone comes from different life experiences and psychological and emotional places. Just because there are things I have discussed in this book doesn't mean they are assumed to be part of your particular struggle. Our work is to learn and understand your own personal situation together and to deconstruct the cycle on a deeper level through our process.

Though I know it may be hard to imagine if you've been entrenched in this cycle, it is possible to overcome this issue. I have seen people overcome Grass Is Greener Syndrome on a regular basis for years. At times it may be challenging, and there may be painful conversations along the way, and there will be some things that take learning how to manage and cope with in a new way. You may even find yourself thinking about things differently and with a new perspective through the work.

For example, many people don't realize that just because you have an urge or craving to run to something else (or from something) doesn't necessarily mean you're in the wrong place now—even if sometimes it could mean that. People sometimes have conflated the feeling of yearning for shiny green grass to mean that the present is not enough. While it may mean something is missing or needs to be understood more, a strong feeling doesn't always need to be followed or acted upon. Feelings can be helpful guides at times in life. But sometimes, for deeper reasons, an alarm can go off within ourselves because of experiences earlier in life that makes running feel necessary. Sometimes feelings are helpful, and sometimes they are old reactions that helped in the past that actually don't serve you well in the present anymore.

Getting Help

Part of the difficulty of getting help with Grass Is Greener Syndrome is that, outside of my writings that have been circulating on the internet, most of this information is not widespread prior to the release of this book. Everything you're reading in this book comes from years of experience in practice with people. The question therefore becomes how to find help that can adequately address the depth and complexity of this issue. There are a few ways to approach this.

First, I do work with people all across the US and internationally on Grass Is Greener Syndrome as well as other specialties. You are welcome to reach out to me to inquire about availability. I always try my best to bring people in right away, knowing the urgency you may be feeling upon reaching out, however at times there may be a waiting list. Send me an email, call, or go through my website to reach out and we'll discuss your situation together (contact info is at the end of this section).

If you have a therapist you are already working with, I have on numerous occasions worked with people who simultaneously maintain another therapy. This is possible to do, if you and your therapist are okay with this setup.

For options outside of seeing me, if you are looking for someone who can at least help address your struggle to some extent, even without grass is greener knowledge, my best recommendation would be to find a relational or contemporary psychoanalytic therapist, or to find a therapist who has been fully trained and seasoned in psychodynamic therapy. Someone with this education, training, experience, and background should be able to help you get to the depth of the general patterns that are happening within your relationships. While they may not address the grass is greener processes specifically, it should at the very least help you look into some of your patterns more in depth. You are also welcome to reach out to me for a referral to someone who might be able to help.

I do at times get calls from people asking if cognitive behavioral therapy (CBT) would be a good way to go. While cognitive behavioral therapy can at times be a helpful adjunct to certain therapies and issues (I also bring in CBT techniques, when helpful, with some of my other specialties), I would actually not recommend CBT for Grass Is Greener Syndrome. CBT tends to be focused towards changing behaviors and thoughts, while spending much less time (if any at all) on the emotional depth, working through the emotional patterns, and understanding the overall relational patterns that create and reinforce the grass is greener cycle. The methods that CBT therapists often employ to help with certain other issues are actually more likely to perpetuate the grass is greener cycle than to help.

In the end, you are in control of the life you want to have. While you may feel powerless in the grass is greener cycle, repeatedly starting over or stuck in between worlds, you can create new paths and find fulfillment. Whichever way you choose to find your path forward, remember, if you've come this far—and if you've read everything in this book—then you have the resilience and curiosity it takes to find your way through the other end of this issue. It's time to bring you out of the cycle so you can have the life you want. Ultimately, the greener grass is the grass you nurture.

How to Contact Me

The best way to reach me is to send me an email or to contact me through my website. If you prefer to call, my phone number is on the website.

Website: https://nathanfeiles.com

Email: Nathan.Feiles@gmail.com

www.ingramcontent.com/pod-product-compliance
Lightning Source LLC
Chambersburg PA
CBHW071530120626
46550CB00006B/2407